look good, feel good, play good

by
maisie skidmore

with
dal chodha
michelle millar fisher
heather radke
samantha n. sheppard
natalie e. wright

dina asher-smith
scout bassett
joan benoit samuelson
sue bird
deyna castellanos
chandra cheeseborough
anna cockrell
shelly-ann fraser-pryce
kirsty godso
xochilt hoover
rayssa leal
tatyana mcfadden
naomi osaka
megan rapinoe
sha'carri richardson
caster semenya
dawn staley

look good, feel good, play good

 Nike apparel

Φ

contents

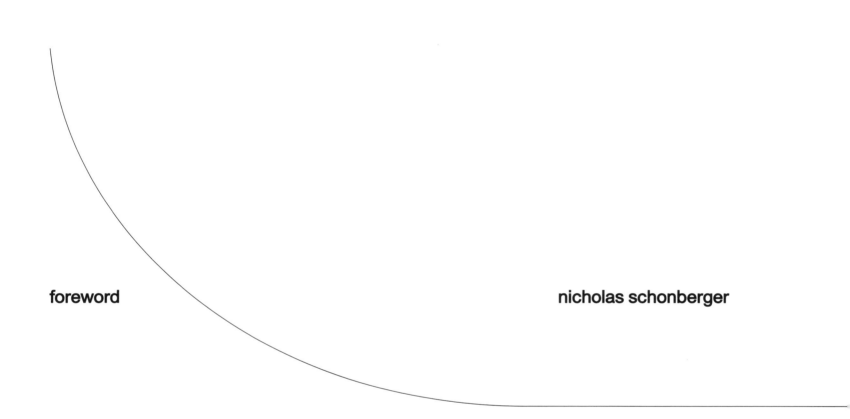

foreword   **nicholas schonberger**

The trajectory of contemporary women's sport runs parallel to Nike's history. Each successive decade from the 1970s bears witness to a revolution. Change moves first at a jog; at times, it sprints; at others, it takes a step back. Shifts in perception—what is possible on roads, fields, and courts—come amid the fluctuations of fitness fads. Whether dribbling, jumping, lunging, running, serving, or stretching, athletes set the standard, calling for new, different, or more, and Nike's designers are tasked with the response.

In many instances, particularly in the early years, athlete and designer are one and the same. Problems experienced are problems solved. Challenges to convention come from the inside, and those challenging are also members of the sporting community. Pushes for progress come from the outside, and those pushing are defining the future of sport.

Look Good, Feel Good, Play Good synthesizes a famous quote from American sporting legend Deion Sanders. The phrase encapsulates a truth for all athletes: success (however defined) requires a balance of body and mind. Athlete anecdotes affirm this premise, and their stories expose a material connection to clothing that transcends style. For all, what is worn, how it is worn, and when it is worn are part of their sporting identity.

This book was conceived, researched, and written from 2022 to 2024. It lands as Nike begins a new chapter of its story, and as new superstars in basketball, football[1], track and field, tennis, and beyond are strengthening television viewership, building fandom, and bolstering a new cross-generational discourse. We ask, how did we get here? Where, and when, has the athletic world crossed over with popular culture? What are the commonalities shared by a full spectrum of athletes? What is constant in what has been worn to train and compete, to run errands, or to work out? How does sport apparel explain where we've been and where we're going?

Exploring answers to these questions highlights continuity in a fluid landscape. Warm-ups, jerseys, leggings, bras, and shorts are always with us. The articulation of these archetypes becomes emblematic of eras. Color, drape, fabric, print, and pattern express period aesthetic values and highlight technical innovations. In these archetypes, we also take in how Nike follows its mantra: "Listen to the voice of the athlete." As individual performance concerns evolve, societal conversations shift, and we embrace life's many stages, garments made for movement are broadened to become strong signifiers of a collective momentum.

introduction   maisie skidmore

Nike's namesake, the Greek goddess of victory, has been captured by sculptors time and again throughout history. Oftentimes in these artworks she is winged, as though about to take flight. Sometimes she is depicted in motion, arms poised to run not away but toward something, her garments loose and flowing behind her. Occasionally she looks out defiantly at her viewer—a woman in triumph, watching herself being watched.

It is fitting that there are many Nike goddesses out there now, exhibited in museums and galleries or held in archives around the world, their faces and figures based on those of real-life models who presumably spent hours posing in dusty ateliers. Each monument embodies a multitude of women all standing for a singular idea: victory.

But if Nike the goddess presents one archetype of womanhood, Nike the brand seeks to support a womanhood that is as pluralistic as possible. Throughout the pages of this book, we share many voices, many stories, many women's perspectives.[2] They are amateurs, champions, trainers, teachers. They are able-bodied and disabled. They push themselves because they want to find out how much they are capable of. It is no secret that women's apparel has not always been a priority for the sporting goods industry. But where sport happens, there Nike is—and there women have always been. What's more, they've always been wearing something. Rather than attempt to rewrite the story, we set out to ask questions. Starting with: what do women wear to move, and why?

Throughout the book, we look at this question through five different lenses, with the collaboration of essayists whose explorations form the framework of our chapters. The first, "Where We Play," considers sporting apparel beyond the court, the field, and the track—tracing athletic performance out onto the street and into everyday life. "Fit Check" examines the power of color and beauty in the context of competition, and the cultural impact of athlete-entertainers performing on what might be the last truly global stage. "The Body: Seen" locates the female form as the object of this global gaze—a machine that is perpetually scrutinized and appraised but also exalted, glorified, and respected. "The Body: Owned" moves beyond what is visible to unpick the themes of empowerment and reclamation, asking what it means for a woman to harness her own strength and what is required from society in order for her to do so. Finally, "Adapt and Evolve" investigates the themes of modification and alteration throughout the history of women's sporting apparel and questions what these experiments might mean for the future of womenswear, both for able-bodied and disabled athletes.

This book has emerged out of an archive, and its images, reproduced as best they can be, are textured, torn, and marked accordingly. Archiving is a radical act. What is saved is remembered; what is remembered becomes history. The Department of Nike Archives (DNA) houses a living collection of objects—clothing, images, ephemera, and more—that charts more than fifty years of design for athletes, thereby creating a blueprint for what comes next. We worked closely with DNA to unearth the artifacts that have defined some of these journeys, choosing to champion not shiny new garments hanging pristine and untouched but the well-worn, the sweat-stained, the ripped, and the exhausted—clothing that has borne witness to greatness.

We also drew on Nike's apparel catalogs—an incomplete collection of precious printed publications documenting what the company made and sold from 1981 until the 2010s. Dubbed "the backbone of Nike's sales force," they are the definitive source of information as far as product lineage is concerned. Tracing the evolution of Nike women's apparel through their pages, a new narrative emerges—one based not on the brand's thoughtfully honed image but on its real relationship with its customers. The material found through this archival research forms our archetypes—a collection of five key items of women's sporting apparel considered throughout contemporary culture. We look at warm-ups, jerseys, leggings, sports bras, and shorts in turn, exploring their evolution and impact on the wider world.

We also pull back from the archive to look at the present day. We share twenty-two accounts from Nike athletes about what they wear to perform—including long-distance runner Joan Benoit Samuelson, sprinter Sha'Carri Richardson, footballer Megan Rapinoe, and tennis player Naomi Osaka. They told stories about the resonance of red lipstick, the power of the bodysuit, the rhythmic bounce of the chain, and the leggings modified to accommodate a prosthetic leg. Time and time again, they said that if they look good, they feel good—and if they feel good, they play good. Precisely what that means is slightly different for each of them—and therein lies the beauty.

For the most part, these women wear what we all wear. At the National Portrait Gallery in London, a 2024 exhibition curated by Ekow Eshun, titled *The Time is Always Now*, presented a study of the Black figure and its representation in contemporary art. Inside the entrance of the show towered a monumental nine-foot-tall bronze statue of a Black woman by British artist Thomas J. Price titled *As Sounds Turn to Noise*. Her image was based on a digitally compiled hybrid of a range of individuals from London and Los Angeles; one person, embodying many different people. Her hands are placed supportively on her hips, chin tilted upward, and eyes closed in thought. Braids cascade down her back. She wears running shoes, ankle socks, a sports bra, and leggings.

She is ordinary—standing as women stand, in the clothes they choose—and yet absolutely extraordinary. She could have been poised to run the race of her life, or to run for the bus that would carry her out of the National Portrait Gallery and away from Trafalgar Square to sail into a mythological future.

On the rainy April morning when I met her at the gallery, I was struck by this monument as an antidote to the vision of Nike the goddess as we know her. The results are in, and she has nothing more to prove to us. She is us. We share her victory.

1

Football has been used throughout to refer to soccer, except in period-specific examples.

2

Throughout this book, we will use the term *woman* to include anyone who identifies as such.

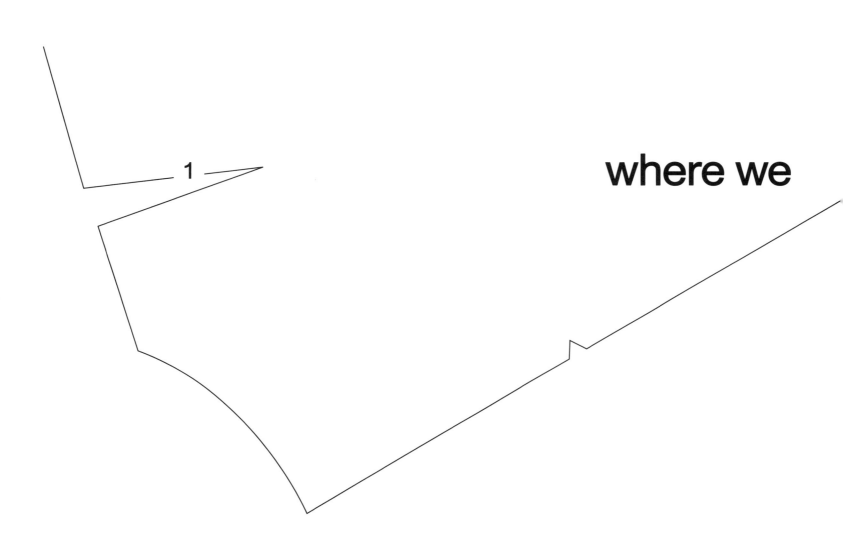

1

where we

play

Sports were jus
Everything coul

t who you were.
d be sportswear.

43

warm-ups

FIG 001

LADY SOFT TOUCH (1553)
85% Arnel Triacetate/
15% Nylon Velour, Raglan
Sleeve, Yoke Front, Welt
Pockets, Rib Cuffs and
Waistband, Pant w./
Drawstring,
Embroidered Logo

FIG 002

Nike officially established its apparel department in 1978, and after more than a decade of producing printed one-pagers showcasing the company's footwear collection each season, it finally had an apparel line to share with retailers. To that end, in 1981 it produced its first ever clothing catalog, "effective for shipments after May 1, 1981," as the subheading claimed. Today, this cream-colored document is a revered artifact.

The catalog is twenty pages long—and the only photographs in it are on the cover, which features twelve cutout images of models gazing happily into the camera. Two pages were dedicated to women's apparel (against nine for menswear, two for youth, and four for accessories). The last of the warm-ups listed in the women's collection was a velour two-piece named Lady Soft Touch. It featured a yoke front, a raglan sleeve, ribbed cuffs, and drawstring pants, and it was available in cool blue, navy, burgundy, and beige. The little illustration doesn't give much away, but product shots from the Department of Nike Archives (DNA) reveal it to be quite timeless, as velour tracksuits go, with a white Nike logo embroidered onto the collar. It looks cozy and comfortable; "sporty" insofar as dressing to make your body feel good is something sporty people do.

By the mid-1980s, both the page count and the production budget for the catalogs had multiplied, with glossy editorial photographs art-directed to show the collections in their best and moodiest light. In the spring 1986 issue, against the backdrop of the studio fitness craze, warm-ups presented a space for experimentation: see the Windstar jumpsuit, for example. It was made from 100 percent nylon ripstop taffeta, with a zip at the front, elastic cuffs and waist, and mesh venting, and it was available in white, tropic blue, and black. Perhaps, as the catalog's photographs suggest, the wearer would pull it on after an aerobics class. She might gossip in the locker room, the jumpsuit rustling softly as she leaned down to pick up her bag.

The early 1990s saw brash colorways, vibrant graphic prints, and spandex unitards, followed later in the decade by a penchant for color-blocked tracksuit tops paired with coordinating tights. These looks had been long forgotten by the early 2000s when everything seemed to shift with a dramatic turn into the new millennium. Suddenly, color palettes, silhouettes, and whole aesthetics turned from busy and bright to muted and cool. In the Spring 2000 catalog, mesh-lined nylon pants were the thing, a drawstring cord at the waist and cargo pockets on the left thigh, in black, white, gray, navy, and perhaps a muted turquoise. They'd be paired, maybe, with a cropped cotton tank top with a hero graphic—and while a matching jacket was an

FIG 003

FIG 004

004

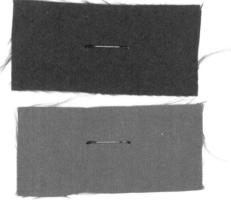

FIG 005

001 Lady Soft Touch, 1981

002 Lady Soft Touch Jacket, 1981

003 Windstar Jumpsuit, 1986

004 Warm-Up front and back sketches by Geoff Hollister, 1980

005 Color nylon swatches from Diane Katz's original Windrunner sketches, 1978

FIG 006

FIG 007

007

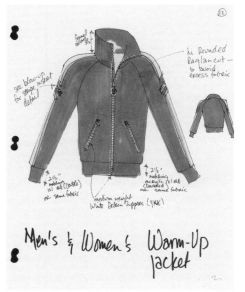

Men's & Women's Warm-Up Jacket

FIG 008

006

Freelance apparel designer Diane Katz and Geoff Hollister, Nike's third employee, collaborated to create the original concept for the Windrunner jacket—a lightweight jacket that would allow runners to keep working out through Oregon's long rainy season. Its chevron was based on the skiwear that Katz had spent several years designing in her role at White Stag; its raglan sleeve was both an economical use of fabric, and a deft way of preventing water from entering at the shoulder seams.

006 Diane Katz modeling an early Windrunner prototype, 1978

007 Diane Katz's first Windrunner sketches, 1978

008 Warm-Up Jacket sketch by Diane Katz, 1978

009 Phil Knight running in Windrunner Jacket, 1979

010 Ladies Windrunner Jacket, 1979

FIG 010

FIG 009

009

option, this was no longer the go-to. These were sportswear-inspired pieces, certainly, but they harbored no lofty ambitions of being worn for sports. But by the 2000s, sports were no longer something you had to dress specifically for; women had been working out without fanfare for twenty, thirty years. Now sports were just who you were. Everything could be sportswear.

As a clothing category, sports apparel performs under extremes of human existence. Warm-ups, however, do not. Warm-ups occupy a liminal space in sportswear that has little to do with performance. They are the nylon tracksuits, the crewneck sweatshirts, the hoodies, the tech fleece. Ostensibly they're designed to be worn right up until the moment of performance, peeled off as it begins, and then pulled swiftly back on once the race, match, or game ends. For some athletes, that really is the case. But for the majority, they serve more as a framing device. They are worn for the trip to or from the gym. They belong not so much to individual sports as to sporting spaces: track, field, pool, gym, football field, tennis court, golf course, tunnel, bench. When you wear warm-ups, you tell everybody you come into contact with that you belong in those spaces, too.

Beyond the sporting arena and its environs, warm-ups form part of a vocabulary of sportsmanship. They are the pre- and post-performance performance—a costume that signals an active life. They are Princess Di in her oversized graphic sweatshirt and cycling shorts, towel slung nonchalantly over her shoulder as she strides purposefully toward the gym. They are the gold medal winner on the medal stand or the sprinter tying their laces one last time on the starting line. They are Rocky Balboa in his heather gray sweats or *Flashdance*'s Alex Owens (played by Jennifer Beals) in her leg warmers. Just as a team jersey, a uniform, or even a band T-shirt is made meaningful by onlookers who understand its connotations, warm-ups crave a spectator perspective that places them within the sporting world.

For those who already have their spectator, warm-ups are part and parcel of the pregame. For professional athletes, the tunnel walk, once the arena of warm-ups, has been hijacked. Now, it's a top-level marketing moment, with fashion brands vying to have their garments photographed as players make their grand entrance before a game. (In contrast, wearing the traditional team-issued sweatsuit in the tunnel can signify that a player is "locked in"—head down, game-ready, prepared for the competition ahead.) And while the clothes themselves have their part to play here, street-style photographers will tell you that they often have little to do with the success of a look. It's the attitude that counts. At its best, it's audacious and at-ease, a slow, unbothered amble through the watching throngs, a gym bag slung nonchalantly over a shoulder. This is "look good, feel good, play good" in action.

If warm-ups are pieces that nod toward a sporting life, they don't end with tracksuits or gym bags. In 1981 Nike produced a collection of sports jewelry that is irresistible for its flashiness. It was available in gold or sterling silver, divided up into Competitor, Pro, and All Star packages—swooshes (aplenty) encircled in metal rings, tiny precious trainers with logos licking the sides, a tennis racket dangling from a metal jump ring. The slogan pendants are the most expressive of all, spelling out the brand's language. Picture the phrase "THERE IS NO FINISH LINE" rendered in block capitals hanging from a gold chain peeking through an open zip collar. Some pieces infer sporting ambition: "SUPER STAR," "CHAMP," "HOT PROSPECT," or the time-honored and not totally modern, "FAST 'N' FOXY." Others, such as "GO FOR IT," capture a more inclusive determination. "This is an exciting new field for Nike, and you can expect this line to reflect the same quality and craftsmanship that [have] become synonymous with all Nike products," the collection description reads. "Each is crafted of the finest materials and styled for a classic *sporty* look." Because what is a "sporty look," and who's to say that it can't be achieved through jewelry?

The term *sporty* casts a wide net—but if you go out looking for it, you'll often find it manifests in layers that can be easily thrown on or peeled off. The history of Nike is indivisible from the climate of Portland, Oregon—well-known for being mild and wet due in part to its proximity to the Pacific Ocean. Rain is expected 154 days a year there, so it makes sense that one of Nike's earliest and most enduring apparel innovations—created in response to a request from Nike employee number three, Geoff Hollister— was a jacket that would provide protection from the elements during the winter training months.

In 1978 Diane Katz became Nike's first professional apparel designer, and she was tasked with responding to the athlete insights that Hollister gathered from a team of Nike-sponsored runners assembled for Athletics West, the running team established by Nike cofounders Bill Bowerman and Phil Knight, along with Hollister in 1977. They wanted training apparel that would keep them warm and dry, allowing them to work out throughout Oregon's long rainy season. Katz, who had designed sportswear for White Stag, had a background in skiwear. But she was also a runner, and told Nike as much.

There was really no such thing as activewear as we now know it in the late 1970s. "This whole category of single, nylon shell jackets did not exist," explained Katz. "There might've been some rain jackets out in the industry for people to wear if they had to stand at a bus stop, but they were so rudimentary." Armed with her expertise, Katz took the traditional ski fabrics that were available to her and used them to create an approachable hooded garment that wouldn't alienate Nike's customers—runners who, most likely, had never before encountered an outerwear garment designed for use while running. She landed on the chevron design because, with its connection to preexisting skiwear styles, it was easy to understand. Paired with the raglan sleeve, which not only allowed for ease of movement but also prevented rain from seeping in through the hardworking shoulder seams, the chevron was a cost-effective approach. "There was no such thing as taped seams or anything in those days," she continued, "and so the height of technology would just be to not have a seam over the shoulder so the water couldn't seep in." Katz was confident it could work.

She was correct. The Windrunner's popularity has seen peaks and valleys over the years—but it has persisted throughout them all. Now, forty-five years after it was first produced, the style exists in both the performance wear (albeit with some technical updates) and lifestyle categories, where it is best known. The vibrant chevron makes it a particularly recognizable piece. In 2008 Katz was stunned to find that competitors from every Nike-sponsored country that took part in the Beijing Olympics wore Windrunners in its country's colors on the medal stand, reviving a style that had been designed thirty years earlier.

Traditionally, a winning athlete wears a medal stand or "presentation suit" to receive their award on the podium. Warm-ups comprise tracksuits and drill suits—all styles that, for the general consumer, translate to windproof and rainproof outerwear. (The Portland DNA is strong.) But the warm-up category also provided

FIG 011

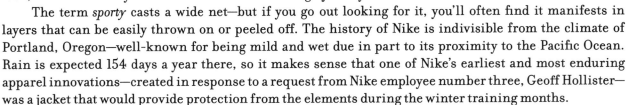

In 1981 Nike produced a collection of sports jewelry—available in gold or sterling silver, and divided into Competitor, Pro, and All-Star packages. Alongside tiny trainers, tennis rackets, and swooshes, slogan pendants featured heavily, ranging from rousing encouragements to the brand's taglines. Inspired though it was, the capsule collection was soon discontinued.

MAN VS MACHINE.

FIG 012

FIG 013

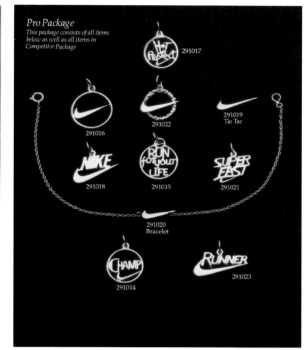

FIG 014

FIG 015

FIG 016

FIG 017

23

FIG 018

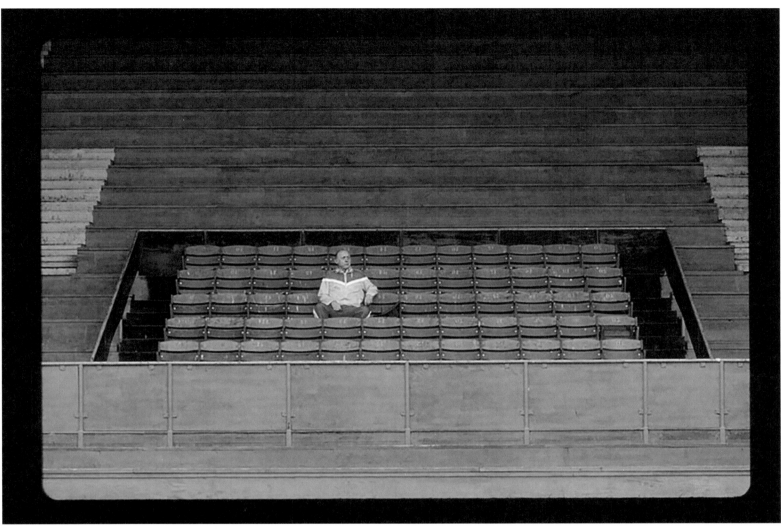

FIG 019

FIG 020

018 "Their Name Is Mud" Poster featuring Lynn Jennings and Pat Porter
wearing Athletics West, 1988

019 Bill Bowerman sitting in box seats at Hayward Field, Eugene,
Oregon, 1982

020 Color nylon swatches from Diane Katz's original Windrunner sketches, 1978

Following spread:

021 Alexis Warm-Up Set, 1982

022 Lady Trainer description in Women's Aapparel Catalog, Fall 1983

023 Lady Season and Lady Triumph in Women's Apparel Catalog, Fall 1983

024 Lady Season and Lady Triumph in Women's Apparel Catalog, Spring 1984

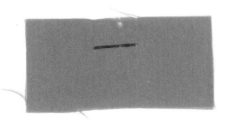

FIG 021

FIG 022

● *1563 Lady Trainer*

Poly/rayon/cotton fleece.
Jacket—Hood with drawstring
and contrast liner, striped cuff
and waistband, raglan sleeve
with accent piped stripe, contrast
full zip, pouch pockets, embroidered logo
Pants—Elastic waist with drawcord, drawcord cuff, embroidered
logo
XS-L
62 **Grey Heather**/Lt. Blue
80 **Grey Heather**/Soft Pink
82 **Grey Heather**/Lilac
91 **Turquoise Heather**/Turquoise
95 **Plum Heather**/Plum

apparel designers with a fertile ground in which to experiment, resulting in the aforementioned Windstar jumpsuit from 1986, for instance. These were pieces that could be audacious, commanding the attention of an opposing team as you stepped down off a bus or warmed up at the side of the field, and symbolizing a readiness to play on removal. They could coordinate with a cohesive tennis-dress look or finish a golf outfit. In basketball, warm-ups included the tearaway nylon pants—a now-iconic design that fastens down the side seams with snaps and is designed to be removed in one rapid ripping motion. Somewhat unexpectedly, and yet brilliantly, they are still in production today.

For some teams, readiness is embodied not by nylon separates but by a smart, tailored two-piece suit. In 2023 Nike turned the notion of the warm-up upside down once again with the help of British designer Martine Rose. Suiting, and subversions thereof, has long been a pillar of Rose's practice, which nods to subcultures from dandies to football hooligans, ravers to northern soulies. Ahead of the 2023 FIFA Women's World Cup, Rose collaborated with Nike to design a collection of unisex tailored suits for the US Women's National Team (USWNT)—and for Nike customers around the world.

So when the team stepped off the bus for the first match of the tournament, they were dressed not in tracksuits but in crisp, navy blue double-breasted suits with matching pants and white buttoned shirts. One side of the jacket bore a patch with the USA logo and stars representing the team's four World Cup wins. On the other was a patch featuring the player's initials. What more powerful way to express the team's shared ambition than with a garment that had so long been designated as "for men"? "When a woman wears a suit, it expresses strength, resilience, and beauty," Rose told Nike. "I want women to feel powerful in their suits like men do. More than that, although I'm using women to tell the story, there's no gender attached to the suit. Anyone can wear it. I hope one day we're not talking about gender in sport and are just talking about the sport. Once everything is stripped back, it's just the game that's left."

For star Megan Rapinoe, wearing it was a powerful experience. "I felt like that was the most amazing gift anyone could ever give me, in my last meaningful games for the national team, to be able to come not in a tracksuit that I didn't feel that good in," she said. "It felt like we were very much a team. It felt almost *Avengers*-like because we had our initials . . . It just felt important. Like we were getting dressed to show up and do our business, and that was part of the pregame. But it was fun to have that too. Tunnel moments have become such a thing, but I've always felt like, you look good, you feel good, you play good."[1]

FIG 023

FIG 024

FIG 025

FIG 026

FIG 027

FIG 028

The Nike Dove Pullover Jacket, introduced in 1983, was part of a series of apparel—light jackets, and shirts with product names such as Lark, Gale, and Meadow. It had a rounded rib collar with a button-down placket, rib cuff and waistband, and zip pocket. It was available in six colorways—including, this lilac hue.

025 Manda Fleece, Fall 1985

026 Stitched Swoosh logo, Fall 1985

027 Cover of Women's Apparel Catalog, Fall 1985

028 Lady Jordan Apparel sketch by Diane Katz, 1985

029 Dove Pullover, 1982

FIG 029

In early 2020 the COVID-19 pandemic shifted the focus of that phrase firmly to "feel good"—where it stayed for several years. With so many people sheltering at home and working from home, warm-ups were thrust into the spotlight. In particular, we turned to tech fleece fabric, a modern, clean, and sleek take on sport fleece, without the traditional brush back or French terry loop backing. In our new and, for many, much more sedentary world, comfort was paramount—but to Nike's eye, the attraction to the sweatsuit was as much psychological as it was physical. Faced with a global health emergency, about which we knew so little, everything was uncertain. Home, for those privileged enough to have one in which they felt safe, became a space of refuge. Sweatsuits provided a refuge within the refuge.

By 2024 the sweatsuit had largely been retired from day-to-day wear, but the warm-up remains. Sportswear and streetwear have always been bedfellows, borrowing freely from one another in the cultural consciousness. As women's professional sports become increasingly visible, women's sportswear is establishing a new space for itself too.

At Nike, the archive still has its part to play, whether that's in the reinterpretation of the Windrunner style or the see-saw between high- and low-rise pants, coordinating and clashing, tight and fitted, or baggy and oversized. But the fun really begins when warm-ups are co-opted by the lifestyle space, and all of the innovation developed for modern performance purposes can be carried over. Fastenings, fabrics, and fits offer versatility. Perhaps a tracksuit top has a double zip so that it can be fastened top to bottom in the cold or worn with both décolletage and belly button on display. Perhaps a long skirt can be zipped off to make a mini, or pants feature bungee cords at the hem, allowing them to be worn wide-leg or tightened to create a balloon silhouette. A jacket might be unzipped at the sides to create space and movement for a full curve, or worn off the shoulder to show some skin. Applying fastenings and technical tricks in these unexpected new styles celebrates the body in a playful way. This approach makes space for body shapes that haven't always been welcomed by sportswear.

And warm-ups are sportswear, certainly. They are made using sports fabrics, in sports shapes, applying sports heritage and sports ideas, to be seen—whether by the audience looking on from stadium seats, millions watching from their sofas at home, passers-by in the street, or neighbors peering out of their window while you take out the trash. But they are not necessarily made for actually doing sports in; they're made for living in.

Sport is play. It's entertainment, competition, determination, and ambition. Sometimes it is victory, oftentimes it's defeat, but it's going back out to give it another go anyway. It's activity, energy, pushing yourself further than you knew you could. In this age we live in, sports have seeped in at the edges of everything we do, and everywhere we do it. Against this backdrop, "look good, feel good, play good" has never felt like such a powerful proposition.

—— 1 ——
Megan Rapinoe, interviewed by the author, January 31, 2024.

FIG 030

*Baseball-type Warm-Up Jacket

FIG 031

FIG 032

FIG 033

GYMNASTICS

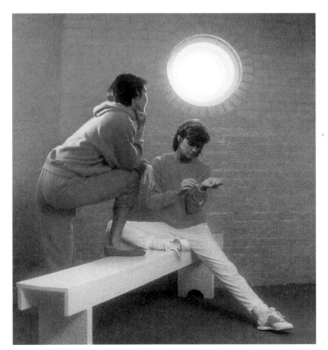

FIG 034

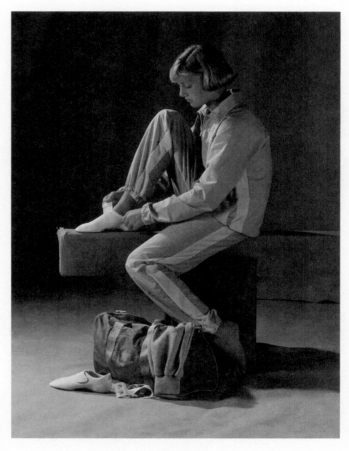

030 Clair Warm-Up Top, 1985

031 Sportswear, 1984

032 Delphi Warm-Up Jacket, 1983

033 Gymnastics Advertising Kit, 1985

034 Solid Fleece Hood, Solid Fleece Crop Pant, Charlotte, and Maryl Pant, Fall 1986

FIG 035

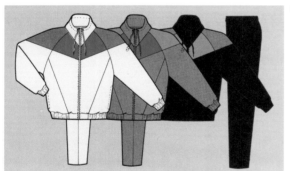

FIG 036

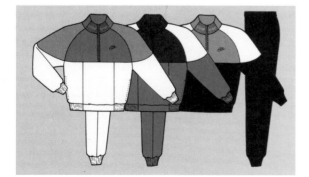

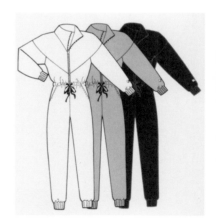

FIG 037

035 Breakdancers, New York City, 1984

036 Half-Zip Warm-Up and V-Line Warm-Up, Fall 1989

037 Lassen, Fall 1986

038 Page from Apparel Catalog, Holiday 1989

039 Knit Twill Warm-Up, Holiday 1988

FIG 038

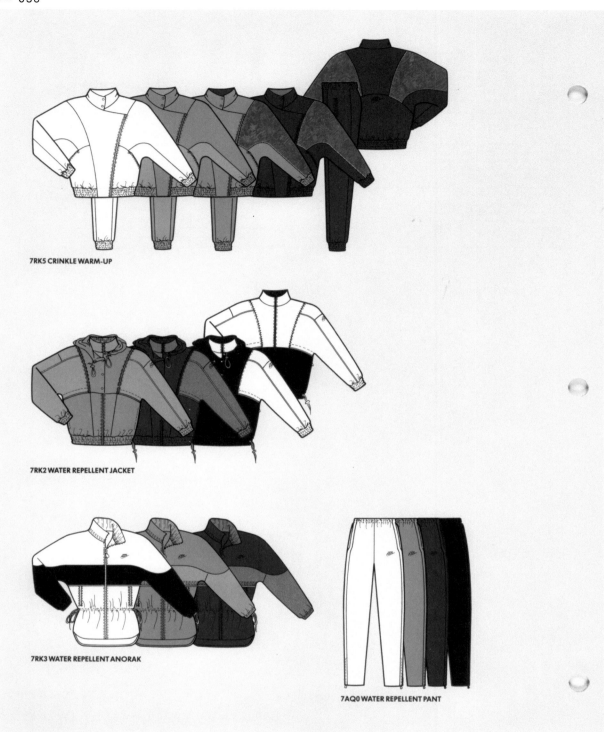

7RK5 CRINKLE WARM-UP

7RK2 WATER REPELLENT JACKET

7RK3 WATER REPELLENT ANORAK

7AQ0 WATER REPELLENT PANT

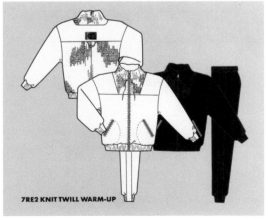

7RE2 KNIT TWILL WARM-UP

FIG 039

FIG 041

FIG 040

041

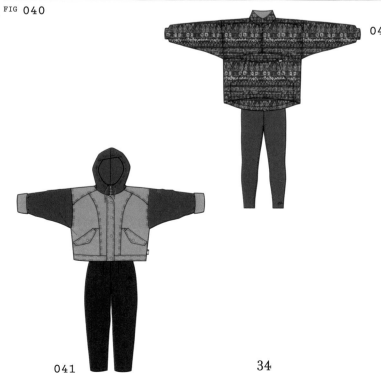

041

041

040 Sylvester Stallone in *Rocky Balboa*, 2006

041 Golf, Gym, Walking, and Active Elements, Fall 1993

042 Page from Apparel Catalog, Holiday 1988

043 Zoom 90 Print Jacket and Zoom 90 Print Warm-Up, Fall 1990

044 Air Jordan Warm-Up Jacket, 1992

041

041

FIG 042

Knit Twill Warm-Up

FIG 043

7BK9 ZOOM 90 PRINT JACKET

7BL7 ZOOM 90 PRINT WARM UP

FIG 044

FIG 045

FIG 046

The Elite Jazz Jacket was released in 1992, during the aerobics craze. Its pattern, which combines flowers with bold stripes and colored grids, was designed by former Nike graphic designer Mary Margaret Briggs. It retailed for $56 USD.

045 Elite Jazz Jacket, 1992

046 Fitness Essentials Warm-Up Jacket, 1992

047 "You Want To Run So Run" Print Ad, 1994

045

you want to run
so run

you want to fly
so fly

you want to be free upon this earth
so be free
be everywhere

and be amazing
as you go

JUST DO IT

FIG 047

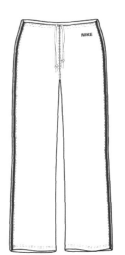

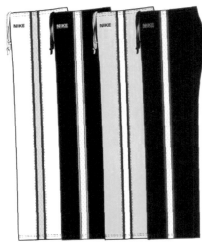

FIG 049

FIG 048

FIG 050

220895

FIG 051

048 "Technology Sets the Spirit Free" Print Ad, 1997

049 City Style Tricot Pant, Spring 2005

050 Jumpman Classic Tear-Away Pants, 2003

051 Basketball Warm-up, Fall 1997

052 Nike Alpine Durasheen Jacket and Nike Alpine Durasheen Pant, Holiday 2005

053 Princess Diana, London, 1995

054 Street Heat Jacket, Funky Fox Ribbed Tee, and Street Heat Pant, Spring 2005

055 Heritage Graphic Tube Top and Heritage Graphic Pant, Holiday 2005

FIG 052

052

FIG 053

FIG 054

FIG 055

054

FIG 056

FIG 057

FIG 058

FIG 059

FIG 060

FIG 061

41

FIG 062

FIG 063

FIG 064

42

FIG 065

066

FIG 066

FIG 067

062 Cover of Women's Performance Apparel, Holiday 2012

063 Serena Holiday Warm-Up Pants, Holiday 2006

064 Serena Holiday Warm-Up Jacket, 2006

065 1980 Olympic Team Windrunner Jacket (detail), 1980

066 Medal Stand Apparel: 21st Century Windrunner, Bowerman Tech Pant, and Flyknit Trainer+, 2012

067 Nike Running Women's Printed Overlay Windrunner, 2014

068 Nike All-Over Print Windrunner, 2014

FIG 068

Nike
Women

NIKE SIGNAL
LONG SLEEVE TEE
Bold style meets
total freedom
with this loose-
cut, flattering
top.

545463-010 (Black/
Sail) XS-XL $40

NIKE RUN LUNAR
TEE
Layer this soft
cotton tee up
or down for
effortless style.

625132- 063 (Dark
Grey Heather) XS-XL
$40

NIKE RUN THE
EARTH TANK
All-day
inspiration,
all-day cotton
comfort.

633081- 455 (Deep
Royal Blue) XS-XL $30

NIKE RUN THE
EARTH TANK
All-day
inspiration,
all-day cotton
comfort.

633081- 063 (Dark
Heather Grey) XS-XL $30

NIKE SIGNAL
LONG SLEEVE TEE
Bold style meets
total freedom
with this loose-
cut, flattering
top.

545483-100 (Sail/
Black) XS-XL $40

NIKE SIGNAL
KEEP ON
KEEPING ON TEE
Classic comfort
and style.

589026-010 (Black)
XS-XL $40

NIKE RUN LUNAR
TEE
Layer this soft
cotton tee up
or down for
effortless style.

625132-010 (Black)
XS-XL $40

NIKE SIGNAL GO
LIKE HELL TEE
Speak your
mind and stay
cool with this
flattering,
loose-cut tee.

633390-632 (Deep
Garnet) XS-XL $40

NIKE SIGNAL
SHORT SLEEVE
TEE
Bold style meets
total freedom
with this loose-
cut, flattering
top.

545483-010 (Black/
Sail) XS-XL $35

Live

FIG 069

FIG 070

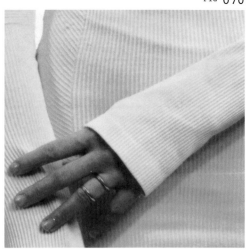

FIG 071

FIG 072

▼ Their accompanying tech sheet describes these women's 2018 Sportswear Pants as "RETRO AND READY FOR FUN." It continues: "Head out in heritage style with the Women's Nike Sportswear Pants. Made with lightweight woven fabric, they feature a striped waistband, a relaxed fit and buttons on the sides for a look full of retro flair...High-waisted design creates a flattering fit. Snap-button closure along the sides provides custom styling. Open side pockets provide convenient storage."

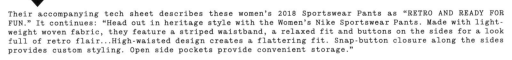

069 Page from Women's Style Guide, Fall 2014

070 Nike Pro Seamless Hyperwarm Hoody (detail), Spring 2014

071 Women's Nike Sportswear Pants, 2018

072 Page from Women's Style Guide, Fall 2014

FIG 073

FIG 074

FIG 075

073 Nike Woven Jacket T2, Fall 2015

074 Logo, Spring 2015

075 Nike Sportswear Windrunner Sherpa Jacket, 2018

076 Martine Rose x Nike, 2018

077 PSG Essential Women's Nike Woven Graphic Jacket (detail), 2022

078 Nike Sportswear Circa 50 Romper, 2022

079 Jordan Brand Winter Utility Collection Campaign, 2020

FIG 076

076

FIG 079

FIG 077

FIG 078

FIG 080

FIG 081

FIG 082

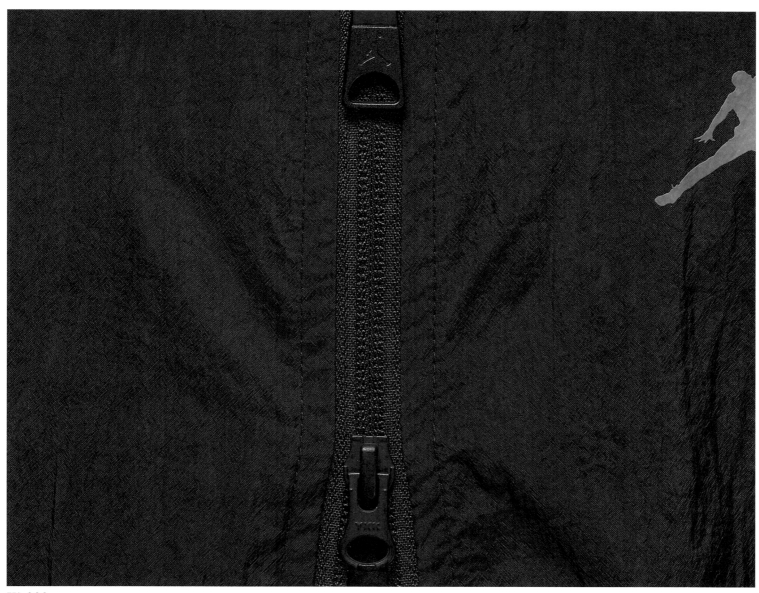

FIG 083

FIG 084

080 Jordan Brand Winter Utility Collection (detail), 2020

081 Nike Sportswear Tech Fleece Women's Oversized Duster Jacket (detail)

082 Nike Team Kenya Shieldrunner Jacket, 2020

083 Jordan Sport Jam Warm-Up Jacket

084 Nike Air Women's Mid-Rise Breakaway Trousers

FIG 085

FIG 086

The tunnel walk, or the route by which an athlete enters the arena before a basketball game, has long provided male athletes with both a major fashion marketing opportunity and a catwalk for exhibiting a broad spectrum of personal style. Now, as the women's game rises in the contemporary consciousness, female athletes are harnessing it, too, demonstrating a new and tangible embrace of athletes as influencers.

085 Alyssa Thomas #25 and DeWanna Bonner #24 of the Connecticut Sun, September 10, 2023

086 Aerial Powers #3 of the Minnesota Lynx, June 9, 2023

087 Satou Sabally #0 of the Dallas Wings, July 9, 2023

088 Jordin Canada #21 of the Los Angeles Sparks, July 31, 2022

089 Jordin Canada #21 of the Los Angeles Sparks, July 9, 2023

FIG 087

FIG 088

FIG 089

FIG 090

FIG 091

090 Nike Plus Size Collection

091 Nike Sportswear Tech Fleece

FIG 092

FIG 093

092

Ahead of the 2023 FIFA Women's World Cup, British-Jamaican designer Martine Rose collaborated with Nike to design a collection of unisex tailored suits for the US Women's National Team (USWNT) to wear as they arrived at the tournament. The collection dissolved the boundaries between men's and women's football styling with a double-breasted jacket featuring each players' initials, matching pants, and crisp white shirts.

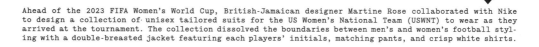

092 Nike x Martine Rose USWNT Collection featuring Megan Rapinoe, 2023

093 Nike x Martine Rose USWNT Collection featuring Crystal Dunn, 2023

094 Lynn Williams, 2023

095 Nike x Martine Rose USWNT Collection, 2023

FIG 094

FIG 095   095   095

June, 1980. Eugene, USA.

Chandra Cheeseborough competes in the 1980 US Olympic Track and Field Trials.

October 20, 1985. Chicago, USA.

Joan Benoit Samuelson crosses the finish line to win first place in the women's division of the Chicago Marathon.

August 24, 2023. Budapest, Hungary.

Sha'Carri Richardson prepares to run in the women's 200-meter semi-finals during day six of the World Athletics Championships.

ATHLETE: CHANDRA CHEESEBOROUGH

SUBJECT: RED LIPSTICK

BIOGRAPHY: Chandra Cheeseborough is an American track and
field athlete and coach, who competed in the 100-,
200-, 400-, 4×100-, and 4×400-meter sprints. She was
born in 1959 in Florida, USA.

Clothes and makeup [are] my thing.

[They make] me feel like I'm ready to step on the track and get it done.

I love lipstick— red, to be exact.

Something that Coach Temple always would say [when we were competing in the late 1970s and early 1980s] was,

'Run like a guy, but look like a fox.'

So we would dress to the nines.

All that comes back into play, ties in with your confidence.

I try to instill that in my student-athletes now.

If you look good, you run good.

ATHLETE: JOAN BENOIT SAMUELSON

SUBJECT: THE SINGLET

BIOGRAPHY: Joan Benoit Samuelson is an American long-distance
runner who competes in the marathon. She was born
in 1957 in Maine, USA.

The fewer layers I'm wearing,

the faster I feel.

So I always train in a t-shirt and race in a singlet.

I leave them for game day, the special kits and the special shoes.

In training, I need to be wearing what's right for the climate and the weather conditions.

When facing competition, I just need to feel as comfortable and as race-ready as I possibly can.

ATHLETE: SHA'CARRI RICHARDSON

SUBJECT: NAILS

BIOGRAPHY: Sha'Carri Richardson is an American track and field athlete who competes in
the 100- and 200-meter sprints. She was born in 2000 in Texas, USA.

I like to express myself.

My nails, you know, these are my babies.

My hair as well. My lip color.

I feel like I got that from being around beautiful women all my life—

an understanding that even if you can't necessarily wear something different, you can still show that you are different.

I feel like my nails do that, my hair do that.

And my pretty face do it too.

If I'm going to present myself in a certain way, I have to be able to back it up.

So if I'm going to look as fierce as I want to, I have to be able to put that performance on as well.

If anything [my look] boosts me.

ATHLETE: DINA ASHER-SMITH

SUBJECT: MAKEUP

Makeup is important when I'm getting ready on race day.

It's both the zoning in, having quiet time alone, and that process of actually executing a look [that] also calms you and focuses you.

When you commit to strong makeup, you're also committing to being seen.

So for me, it's a sign of commitment.

It's about how it makes me feel, or the energy it brings out of me, rather than what it looks like.

When you're on track, all of this stuff disappears.

When I'm in race mindset, I will not care what I look like—the job is to win, and that's that.

But for me, it is a performance.

At the end of the day, we are entertainers.

ATHLETE: ANNA COCKRELL

SUBJECT: SERENA WILLIAMS'S MINISKIRT

BIOGRAPHY: Anna Cockrell is an American track and field athlete who competes in the
              100- and 400-meter hurdles, and the 4×400-meter sprint. She was born in 1997
              in California, USA.

Serena Williams at the [2004] US Open in that denim Nike miniskirt fundamentally altered my brain chemistry.

I was seven years old, and I was a miniskirt girl after that.

I remember that being a big moment for me, seeing that melding of streetwear and sports and performance.

Would I wear a miniskirt to the track?

No, because that's not really in my style now.

But for finding a way to bring elements of my personal style into my own sporting career, Serena doing that was a pivotal moment.

The audacity of it was amazing to me.

How different it was from what anyone has worn, before or since.

Tennis is very traditional, and there was the willingness and the bravery to lean in to your own style in this sport.

That's what it is to be your own person—to know who you are and to stand on it at all times.

And the lace-up and the shirt? Oh my God.

Still to this day, I'm like, what a look.

What a look.

where

we play

dal chodha

What clothes does the body need when it has become a modem made of skin and muscle? So much of our existence, our way of living, is as a physical body attuned to the hundreds of events, actions, and prompts contained in the palms of our hands. Although I am meant to be writing about the places in which sporting clothes or sporting attitudes appear—on your office stairs, in nightclubs, on TV, or anywhere *but* the sports field—I was struck by how much this woman's clothes turned the worn rubber under her feet and the graying walls surrounding her into a strangely suspended space. These were clothes difficult to label, worn in a place that is an aggregate of the countless ways we exist in the world. I was witnessing a way of dressing that was formally unclassifiable, unanxious, and ultramodern—at a point between what *was*, what *is*, and what *will be*.

Since the mid-twentieth century, the increasing sportification of women's clothing and style has asserted a desire and demand for comfort and agility. Feminists of the eighteenth and nineteenth centuries recognized that physical strength and the right to exercise were issues for women. They would become a gateway to some kind of equality. Claire McCardell, the American designer credited as being the "creator of women's sportswear," wrote in her 1956 book *What Shall I Wear?*, "I like to be able to zip my own zippers, hook my own eyes. I need a dress that can cook a dinner and then come out and meet the guests." It is a request that seems absurd to us today, yet McCardell's legacy is in her teachings on how clothes that are dictated by fashion often obfuscate the body with their frills and buckles, patterns, and embroideries. They get in the way of life.

Fashion clothes—with their shine or slack or spikes—are playfully deployed to delineate time, place, and space. Photographs of Kristen Stewart signing autographs while wearing a beaded Roberto Cavalli gown with a pair of Nike trainers at the UK premiere of *The Twilight Saga: Breaking Dawn Part 1* in 2011 concede to the need for comfort, but they are also an exhibition of female agency. The paparazzi seized upon Princess Diana numerous times on her way into the gym, keys in her mouth, wearing roomy sweatshirts and Lycra cycling shorts, clutching a bamboo-handled canvas Gucci bag. She's frozen in those pictures, both on and off duty—free from the formalities of her job for a moment. She is caught between the palace and Pilates in an echo of Sylvia Plath's "pain, parties, work" loop, as described in the poet's journals.

The clothes women wear today—their cut and their drape and, more so, their attitude—reflect a sporting life. Although McCardell's clothes were not specifically designed for playing sports (women in the 1950s did not seem ever to sweat or tire), in her wardrobe was a solution to the busying of lives: clothes appropriate for the office, cocktail hour, and leisure activities all at once. They were essentially the "athleisure" of their time—a means of dressing for an ample life.

Sporting activity is often bookended by another kind of motion: we go to the gym before heading to work, or we work at the gym. We might go to see friends for lunch after yoga, or we might FaceTime them from the café next door. Stretched leggings, sculpted hoodies, pleated jerseys, nylon blousons, thick socks, and bags slung across the body fundamentally demand comfort and yearn for purpose.

Speaking to US *Vogue* about the new sporty style for the American woman in January 1994, the indomitable Isaac Mizrahi claimed the penchant for athletic fashions was "about gyms and running and people exercising, but it [was]

Your heart is beating.
This means you are alive.
Your body is moving.

A sweating, pensive real-life goddess of Nike was purposefully striding on a treadmill at mid-speed in my local budget gym this morning. Her attention was split among an iPad playing a Netflix documentary with subtitles on, a dimly lit smartphone clutched in her right hand, and her own reflection in the full-length mirror lining the walls. This was a young woman suspended in a life both real and phantasmic.

Dressed in high-waisted leggings, a one-shoulder matching top, thick cream-colored socks, and bright white sneakers, she was at ease in the space between the corporeal and the aerial. She was a woman accompanied, as the art critic and novelist John Berger observed, "by her own image of herself."[1] She was at the gym in sports clothes, but she was also in Mexico City via her iPad while also speaking to a friend, who could have been five streets away, on her phone.

She was everywhere all at once.

— 1 —
John Berger, *Ways of Seeing* (London: British Broadcasting Corporation and Penguin Books, 1972), 46.

also about wearing the most comfortable clothes in the world." The mood was mirrored by a campaign that Nike ran at the time that equated working out with falling in love: "The idea was not to make the ad so sports-specific," explained Nancy Monsarrat, divisional advertising manager at Nike at the time. "We're widening the net by leaving the interpretation open-ended, so you could relate it to a relationship or an athletic activity. It's just more about life."[2]

Life today might entail running a business from a kitchen table, doing the school run, shopping for vegetables or wrenches or cars, meeting friends for lunch, or working at a blond lacquered desk in a glass-lined office—all of this can be interpreted as the sport of living.

It's a shame that the existentialist philosopher, writer, and thinker Simone de Beauvoir wasn't alive to appraise the maniacal, magical offering of pre-millennium female archetypes the Spice Girls. I think she would have gotten a kick out of seeing Sporty Spice backflip through the carpeted lobby of London's Midland Grand Hotel crooning, "Slam your body down and wind it all around!" wearing a blistering fluoro-orange halter neck crop top and Yves Klein-blue tracksuit bottoms in the goofy music video for their debut single "Wannabe," released in 1996.

Throughout their career, the Spice Girls—Ginger, Scary, Posh, Baby, and Sporty—gushed with the vim and adventure that de Beauvoir advocated for in her groundbreaking work of feminism, the two-volume *The Second Sex* (1949), published nearly five decades earlier. The group yelled, thrust, and winked a new, pluralistic feminism into the late 1990s, flinging themselves across popular culture in gymnastic frenzy. In her chapter "La jeune fille" ("The Young Girl") in *The Second Sex*, de Beauvoir wrote that girls should "swim, climb mountain peaks, pilot an airplane, battle against the elements, take risks, go out for adventure, and she will not feel before the world timidity." Clothes that have borrowed their attitude from sportswear respond and adapt to a multitude of scenarios and femininities. Whether in Baby's *Valley of the Dolls* kittenishness, Posh's knowing vertiginous heels, or Sporty's Olympian poise, the Spice Girls signaled the gall and liberty of new-millennium femininity—"a weird mix of tomboyish athleticism and coquettish seduction," Joy Press freaked out in the *Village Voice*.[3]

If the new millennium brought with it a buzzy optimism toward technology, society, and politics, then the Spice Girls were promoters of a new, looser, and less academic feminism: "Each of us wants to be her own person and, without snatching anyone else's energy, bring something creative and new and individual to the group. We're proof this is happening," Ginger told the punk writer Kathy Acker in 1997.[4] "When the Spice Girls first started as a unit, we respected the qualities we found in each other that we didn't have in ourselves. It was like, 'Wow! That's the Spicey life vibey thing, isn't it?'" The Spicey life vibe was one full of activity and ambition, grit and sweat, and mascara. It presented the real world as imagined by the young girls in Nike's pioneering "If You Let Me Play" campaign, which had debuted just two years earlier in 1995. "If you let me play sports, I will like myself more," it began.

The Spice Girls were willing pinups for a femininity that tore apart the suffocating gaze of men. Their dissident mash-up of normative clothes was an attempt to represent the everywoman in all her abundance. With her strong body and unabashed nimbleness, Sporty Spice was an icon of athleticism and a goddess of independence.

This idea of a sporting life—one in which young girls become women who are in control, choosing to work, raise families (or not), look after themselves

The clothes women wear today—

their cut and their drape and, more so, their attitude—

reflect a sporting life.

— 2 —

Katherine Betts, "Fashion: Fashion Pumps Up," *Vogue*, January 1994.

— 3 —

Joy Press, "Notes on Girl Power," *Village Voice*, September 23, 1997, www.villagevoice.com/notes-on-girl-power.

4

Geri Halliwell, interview by Kathy Acker, "All Girls Together," *Guardian*, May 1997, www.theguardian.com/music/2018/feb/26/when-kathy-acker-met-the-spice-girls.

first and then one another, all while jumping over hurdles and into cars, over puddles, and into virtual worlds—has changed how women dress.

We're all cyborgs disguised under piles of organic matter. The clothes that have evolved to suit women's lives today are responding to this change as we jog with smartwatches monitoring our breath. We record our sleep with aluminum phones underneath feather pillows. We download apps to monitor our organs, and we each surveil the bodies of women, zooming in on the millions of pictures posted each second of every day.

A face squashed into the palm of a hand, a thumb scrolling, and a pencil being dragged across the pages of a sketchbook. A long puffer jacket billowing in the wind outside a coffee shop. The ears twitching to the crunch of a nylon jacket. The jolt of electric feedback of a polyester fleece. Sports clothes are all around us, spectators to a life of hyper-digital connectedness that feels at once comforting and completely and utterly terrifying. Hunched over laptops for most of the week, we seek a comfort that anonymizes the body. One that makes its bulges and aches much softer and less noticeable. This is the legacy of sporty clothes. They cocoon a body that is becoming useless. They support a body that needs a push notification to remind it to move.

If you were traveling by train to the city of Nara in Japan to meet a friend at some point between the late 1980s and early 2000s, it's likely you were told to meet them beneath a 10¾-foot (3.3-meter) tall replica of the *Nike of Samothrace*. Originally made for Nara's *Silk Road Exposition* of 1988, the sculpture was no doubt witness to the evolving athleticism of women's dress and the mood for clothes that were not casual, not formal, not in combat but definitely in motion.

Imagine the groups of school friends below the blueish lights of Nara station, huddled at the foot of the goddess as they planned shopping trips in nearby Osaka. The travelers checking timetables, reading newspapers. The surrounding fluorescent kiosks selling magazines, fried snacks, and fizzy drinks. Imagine the mothers pushing their newborn babies around the statue, lulling them to sleep as the din of people rushing about soothed their cries. And the grandparents reading their books nearby. Imagine the pure camp of this masterpiece of Grecian art redone in resin and placed into the center of a Western-style building in the middle of Japan.

The goddess Nike, with her victorious, confident stance, windblown, draped clothes, and strong body, is both a woman on the move and a woman in repose—a constant spectacle of power and prowess. In her stillness, she is an avatar of movement and force. Nike named itself after this woman.

When the construction of a new station building began at Nara in 2003, the goddess spent some years wrapped in sheets of brown cardboard. She was then moved to a local school, where, at the time of this writing, she remains at the foot of the staircase leading to the library. Also in 2003, photographer Danielle Levitt began a photo series for *Vice* of women who were embedded within the ripe UK garage music scene, with its percussive beats and glitched rhythms. Levitt's pictures capture a group of athletic women whose combat happened on the dance floor at the Twice As Nice club night on a Sunday. She places them on the pavement of their local streets at dusk.

Levitt's career began with the street-style pictures she took in New York City in the late 1990s. Around the early 2000s, she started to build a body of work that captured the diverse and complex subcultures of the young people she met and presented them in contexts that helped to frame their clothes. The resulting monograph, *We Are Experienced*, has become a prescient guide to the changing notions of youth culture. In a tree-lined suburb of Jackson, New Jersey, a young teen stands unsure in a fresh raspberry pink velour tracksuit, channeling the entitled sloth-glamour of hotel heiress Paris Hilton. In Scotland, four windswept hockey players drape themselves over a flagstone wall in harlequin jerseys and muddied socks. In California, a distracted girlfriend or sister wears a cropped sports jersey with the number thirteen on it and picks her toes.

Levitt places her subjects into their own environments, and so these spaces—the rubbish-strewn rooms, the wintery streets, the garish gardens—are meant to offer us context, or confirmation, on the construction of identity and style.

In researching women's clothes and the places that sportswear hides in plain sight, I discovered a black-and-white picture shot by the Ghanaian-Russian photographer Liz Johnson Artur from a wider series chronicling nonbinary Black life in London around 2018. In it, the astral, multihyphenate performer Ms. Carrie Stacks is a goddess disheveled. Seemingly taken in the early hours, one imagines after a night out, the photograph shows her in a lift with a friend, her hand stopping the lift door from closing on Artur. The heels are off. The eyelashes are still on. The electrified Nike swoosh licks the bottom of the frame. It is an image charged with transitional and transitory magic. In the intensity of their gaze, Stacks and her friend are athletic, standing present between worlds.

Athletic women understand that every aspect of life can be played or lived out like a sports match. Sportswear is not only for athletes but also for the everywoman, every day. The prevalence of athletic details increasingly found in women's wardrobes comes at a time when our bodies are becoming more sedentary; yoga wear is worn for the training of the body but also the at-home work session that follows it. As the mind has expanded in a million different directions, we have had to cultivate a new understanding of our limbs, our breath, our muscles, and our skin. These new play clothes epitomize the binaries of modern living.

I started to write down things I would see on my daily walk around London—things that had a sporting attitude, not exclusively a sporting look: A nylon bomber jacket with heavy plastic teeth–zipped pockets worn with a neat merino knit jumper. Thick loopback jersey jogging bottoms tucked into white socks and worn with patent leather court shoes with fat bows on the front. A baggy cashmere jumper, the sleeves drooping and bunched up at the elbows, an arched back peering into a computer screen. A raglan sleeve. A ruched circle of elastic around the hip. A pair of legs folded underneath a body, a laptop perched on a knee. A large T-shirt with the sleeves rolled up and out of the way. A mother pushing a pram down a busy street. A group of friends sitting on the grass in a cold park. A woman running to school, to work, and back again while running a business from her phone. Each of these scenarios channels the energy, intention, and physicality of the goddess Nike herself, who is there as a statue in Nara and at the top of the grand Daru staircase at the Louvre Museum in Paris, at the queue in Whole Foods, at the rubbish tip, making lunch in the kitchen. Swiping her mouth with lipstick. Stretching her arms, craning her neck. She's there in all women of today.

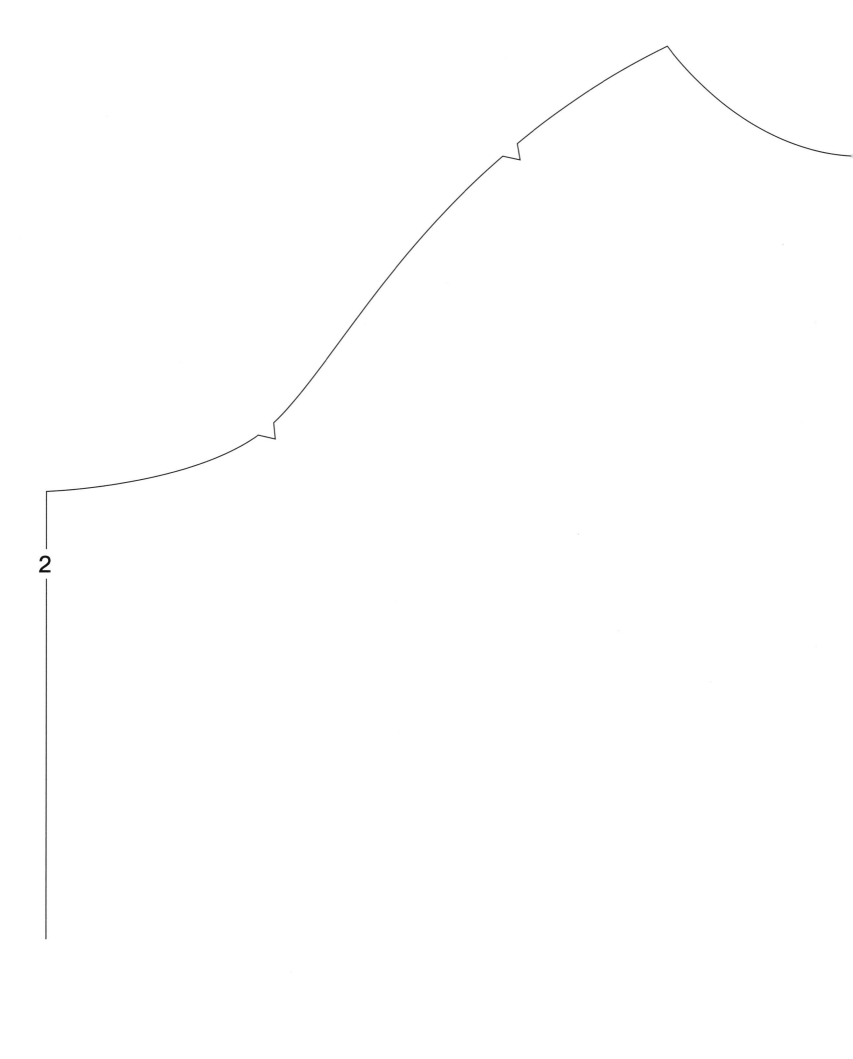

2

fit check

Style objects,

symbols of attitude and affiliation.

jersey

FIG 096

096

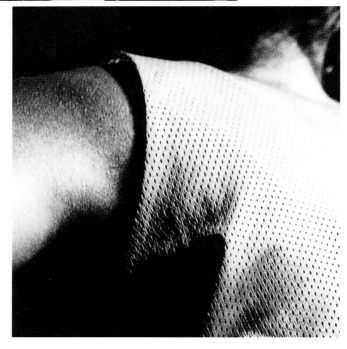

096

FIG 097

FIG 098

FIG 099

▼

"She is eight feet tall," read the original copy on this ad for the Air Flight Deny basketball shoe, featuring Dawn Staley (who, in fact, measures up at a mere 5 foot 6 inches). Released in 1997, the ad followed a gold medal performance with Team USA at the 1996 Atlanta Olympics. Staley was playing in the American Basketball League with the Richmond Rage at the time, two years before the WNBA played its first game.

096 "We Are the Stories We Tell" featuring Lisa Leslie (detail), 1997

097 USA 1996 Atlanta Olympics Basketball Jersey autographed by Sheryl Swoopes, 1996

098 USA 1996 Atlanta Olympics Basketball Jersey autographed by Dawn Staley, 1996

099 Air Flight Deny in "She is Eight Feet Tall" featuring Dawn Staley (detail), 1997

"Once upon a time, three girls went to Rock Steady for a pickup game," Spike Lee's familiar voice intones as the camera pulls in, satisfyingly grainy, on three women—Lisa Leslie, Sheryl Swoopes, and Dawn Staley—walking down a Manhattan street. It's a bright day, and they're dressed casually in blues and reds; their T-shirts are big and baggy, the wide armholes of their oversized jerseys exposing the flash of a sports bra or a vest underneath. "Yo!" Lisa Leslie calls out, statuesque and now at ease on the court. "We got next!"

In 1995, when Spike Lee directed this thirty-second spot for Nike, women's professional basketball was already well established in Europe, but the stability of its future in the United States was uncertain. Up until this point, it had been an amateur pursuit, whether at a collegiate or Olympic level. The 1990s broke this perspective wide open. Leslie, Swoopes, and Staley were about to embark on a groundbreaking nine-month, fifty-two-game exhibition tour in preparation for the 1996 Olympics in Atlanta, Georgia, at which the USA would take home gold for both women's basketball and women's football. The Games would be referred to as the "Summer of the Women"[1]—but it was that preceding tour that truly changed the game for women's basketball. The team's success on the road was galvanizing; the Women's National Basketball Association (WNBA) was founded one year later, in April 1996, with play beginning in 1997.

This ad, titled "Pick-Up Game," features the aforementioned trio of Leslie, Swoopes, and Staley taking on a team of male players at the famous Goat Park court at West 98th Street and Amsterdam Avenue in New York City. It's a joy to watch precisely because pickup basketball is the world that these female athletes were born out of; they had no need for signature shoes, performance wear, or dressing rooms—only cotton, asphalt, and a willing competitor. They call out to one another breezily as they dribble and pass and shoot. "And this isn't a fairy tale," Lee's voiceover continues, "so they didn't beat every guy. But they beat enough to say basketball is basketball, athletes are athletes."

The 1990s marked a turning point for women's sports more broadly, as institutional recognition began to create space for the making of celebrities. Women's basketball was not a young game; its inception had come in 1892 at Smith College in Massachusetts, one year after the first men's game was played there.[2]

FIG 101

FIG 100

You Go, Girls!
The U.S. Women's Basketball Team
(From left: Sheryl Swoopes, Katrina McClain, Ruthie Bolton, Lisa Leslie, Teresa Edwards, coach Tara VanDerveer)

(At the time, women competed in floor-length skirts, no less.) In women's football, the first official women's World Cup took place in 1991, after a handful of guerrilla and prototype versions were held from Mexico City to China. (The first recorded women's match had happened 110 years earlier, in 1881.[3]) But professionally it took time, money, and exposure to propel women's teams to the forefront of the national consciousness. Nike saw ways to support women's teams in, for example, ad campaigns, commercials, endorsement deals, and the first women's signature basketball shoe (Air Swoopes), building the kinds of foundations on which tangible fandom grows. But there was another facet that would be equally impactful—a keystone for team sports, and one altogether more accessible for an apparel company: the jersey.

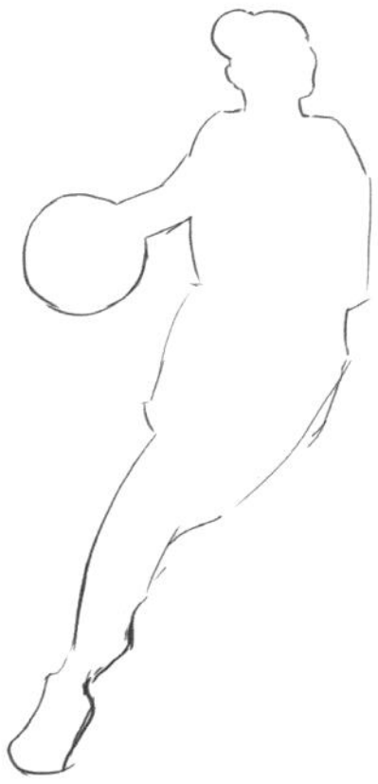

A sports jersey is an icon of athleticism, a visual motif around which contemporary culture creates a whirlwind of energy. It employs graphic design in its color palette, typography, and logo, and clothing design in its every stitch, seam, and detail. When sports stores started selling replica jerseys in the mid-1970s, the door was opened for every fan to step inside the skin of their favorite player and to advertise their fandom to the world around them. These are not pieces purchased for playing in, necessarily; they are style objects, symbols of attitude and affiliation. If you've ever bought or worn one, had your name heat-pressed onto the back, doodled a team mascot, or avoided certain colors, you'll know. Sports jerseys are thick with meaning; they are talismans of fandom.

When it comes to the women's jersey, however, building that heritage is sometimes still a work in progress. Women's team sports are often younger; in many cases, a women's team has little choice but to piggyback off a preexisting identity developed for their male counterpart. In decades past, the sporting world has only really seen a sprinkling of female players establish themselves as household names. However, the numbers are increasing and women's team sports are becoming a talking point not only once every four years but season after season.

This is where the jersey comes into its own. The narrative that underpins fandom is born out of individual moments of greatness, rivalries, underdogs, style, and sensation. But the jersey is the visual vehicle

FIG 102

FIG 103

FIG 104

100 *Sports Illustrated* Olympic Preview Issue, 1996

101 Nike / WNBA Logo

102 WNBA Logo sketches, 2019

103 "Questionnaire" featuring Sheryl Swoopes, 1993

104 "Basketball Is Basketball. Athletes are Athletes." featuring Sheryl Swoopes, 1996

FIG 105

FIG 106

---

105 Portrait of early american basketball teammates, c. 1897

106 "We Don't Think Women Should be Stuck with a Man's Basketball Shoe,"
1978

107 The Game Women's Street Ball Poster, 1985

108 Collegiate Dri-FIT Game Top and Collegiate Dri-FIT Game Short,
Holiday 1998

FIG 107

FIG 108

that carries the narrative from person to person, place to place. When it's good and the conditions are right, the story spreads like wildfire. In jerseys, contemporary apparel designers have the opportunity to be part of building the culture from the ground up. To design one is an honor, a privilege, and a challenge. The designers' goal: to create a garment that stands out as an icon, creates fans, and will still feel sharp in five, ten, twenty-five years' time. Their approach: to look at everything that a team already represents.

Designers think about a basketball team through three lenses: court, community, and culture. The first strand, court, refers to the story that emerges out of the team itself. It is about the heart. What is the history? What have the championship wins been? Who are the key players? The second, community, takes one step back to think about a team within its local context. What does basketball mean to this city? What is the team's story within this community? What is the language they all share? Culture, finally, is where it really gets interesting, pointing a wide-angle lens at what's happening outside of the sport. There's an "if you know, you know" element at play here. The cultural story is about drawing in audiences that exist beyond the parameters of the industry; it taps into something bigger than a court or a community, instead looking outward at the contemporary moment.

The elements the design team has to work with to help perform this feat of cultural construction are wonderfully limited. Color is often tied inextricably to teams, so it's the subtle shift—an almost imperceptible update to a beloved shade, or the reintroduction of a long-forgotten hue—that tends to take the headlines. The jersey's number, serious and sentimental, is crucial; it speaks to tradition and pays homage to others who have worn it in the past. It needs to allow spectators in the nosebleeds to discern what is happening on the field far below, so visibility is paramount. Can jersey numbers be read at a glance from five or five hundred feet away? How do they appear in photographs and on TV screens? Sublimation, embellishment, graphic details, and textures are the tools of the trade. Sometimes, a design team is responsible for gently encouraging an owner, a team, or a league that's reluctant to make a change. Shifts can take time. It's all part of the fun.

Naturally, though, at Nike, the storytelling is only half of the equation. While a jersey needs to look amazing for athletes performing on a world stage, it also needs to feel equally amazing, supporting athletes to move in whichever way they need to. Designing a jersey for women means designing with layering in mind. Like the men's, the women's jersey is often created to work in harmony with a player's shorts or pants, so that the two pieces perform almost as one. Unlike the men's jersey, however, the women's is also created

FIG 109

1-800-650-6936

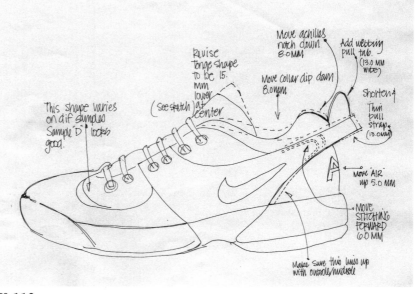

FIG 110

109 Air Swoopes in "1-800-650-6936" 1996

110 Air Swoopes Line Drawing by Marni Gerber, 1993

FIG 111

FIG 113

FIG 114

NIKE

VARSITY BLUE ROYAL 40R / BLACK / COLLEGE RED (IN
BLACK "BASE", WHITE 3/8" : COLLEGE RED "AIRSWOOPES"

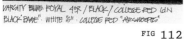

FIG 112

FIG 115

women's
pro
series

▼

This Nike poster from 1997 features All-WNBA first-team selections: Eva Nemcova of the Cleveland Rock-
ers, Ruthie Bolton-Holifield of the Sacramento Monarchs, Tina Thompson of the Houston Comets, and Lisa
Leslie of the Los Angeles Sparks.

111 All-WNBA First Team Poster (detail), 1997

112 Sketch by designer Marni Gerber for the Nike Air Swoopes, the first
signature basketball shoe for a woman athlete, 1995.

113 Page from Women's Apparel Catalog (detail), Summer 1996

114 Dri-FIT Shimmer Game Tank and Dri-FIT Shimmer Game Short, Summer 1999,
and Dri-FIT Game Top, Fall 1999

115 Women's Pro Series Poster (detail), 1998

114

FIG 116

FIG 117

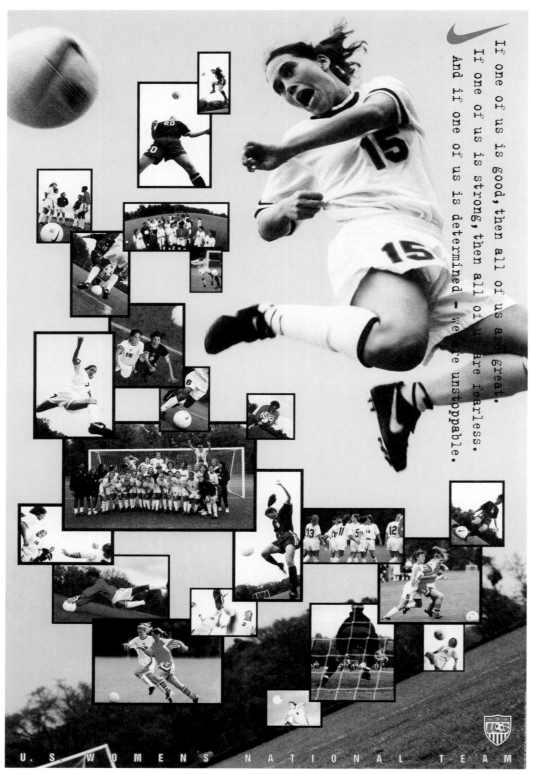

FIG 118

FIG 119

FIG 120

FIG 121

250311-100
250305-010

FIG 122

250152-100

250151-100

116 "Mia Hamm Doesn't Play Soccer For The Glory" featuring Mia Hamm (detail), 1995

117 US Women's National Team Soccer Poster, 1995

118 Mia Hamm's US Women's National Team Jersey for the 1996 Atlanta Olympics, 1996

119 "The US Team Isn't Going To Sweden for the Frequent Flier Miles" (detail), 1995

120 Global Short-Sleeve Jersey, Fall 1996

121 Global Short-Sleeve Jersey and Game Soccer Short, Holiday 1997

122 Women's Nike USA Tee and Women's Nike USA Embroidery Tee, Spring 1996

to work in harmony with the sports bra. Designers prioritize zero-distraction finishes inspired by advances made in undergarment design to ensure that the next-to-skin sensation that occurs around the neckline, armhole, or wrist, is the very best it can be.

Today, innovations in fit, material, and construction mean that the garment is performing at an extraordinarily high level. The results become tangible through wear-testing—a rigorous and extensive process. At this stage, ease, fit, coverage, and comfort are the four key concerns, as the reality of an individual athlete's preference comes into play. Different sports and different people lean toward different sizing, for example—and no matter how effectively a designer can demonstrate that the recommended fit is, say, close to the body, it may be that an individual player simply wants to wear it oversized. Perhaps this is because on the court or on the field, unlike so many other spaces in modern life, women are permitted to—even encouraged to—take up space. There are precise and personal ideas about drape and slouch, and it's up to the designer to accommodate those preferences, sizing up and down and adjusting the fine details based on those changes. This is precisely the push and pull that makes the elite jersey so special; soul becomes a key component of design. As the Nike garment label attests: "Engineered to the exact specifications of championship athletes." When it comes to team sports, style and culture are woven into the fabric of the jersey.

It's important to state, though, that it wasn't always this way. In almost every discipline—be it football, basketball, baseball, softball, ice hockey, field hockey, cycling, and so on—female athletes have historically worn scaled-down men's garment designs. Take football, for example: When Nike signed the US women's team in 1994, one of its key concerns was to upgrade the product available to its players. Nike designers sat down with the team to inquire about their personal preferences, and the athletes were stunned. "I remember them . . . not just sitting me down but talking to all the players . . . and saying, 'How do you like your sweats to fit? Your short length? What thickness of sock do you prefer?'" Mia Hamm tells Nike in "The Women's Movement," a research document produced by the company in 2012 to review its relationship with women athletes. "That made a huge impact on all of us. We were being taken seriously as a national team, wearing a women's cut." (Resourcing for women's football is an ongoing process, and 2019 marked another key moment. Not least because Nike outfitted fourteen of the twenty-four teams who competed in the Women's World Cup that year—and for the first time, each uniform was designed specifically for them, rather than being a derivative of the men's uniforms.[4])

FIG 123

FIG 124

FIG 125

Mia Hamm, professional soccer player

FIG 126

FIG 127

124

123 US Women's National Soccer Team 1996 Olympics, 1996

124 Mia Hamm in action 1996 Olympics, 1996

125 "Protect the Original Intent of Title IX" featuring Mia Hamm (detail), 2006

126 "Europe, Asia & Latin America" (detail), 1996

127 Mia Hamm - US Jersey, Holiday 1997

FIG 128

FIG 129

FIG 130

FIG 131

FIG 132

FIG 133

FIG 134

FIG 135

FIG 136

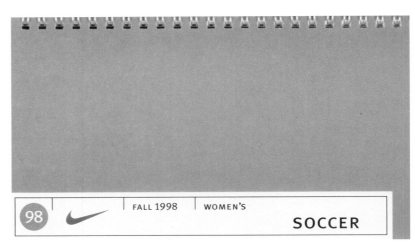

250219 WOMEN'S U.S. TEAM JERSEY

CONTENT: 100% Dri-F.I.T. polyester piqué.
PROFILE: Relaxed fit, short-sleeve rib V-neck with open hem, rib inset at armholes, Swoosh design trademark embroidered at lower right sleeve, Team Sports woven label at lower left front hem, U.S. National Soccer emblem at center front, woven tab label at lower right side seam.
WHOLESALE: $30.00 **SUGGESTED RETAIL:** $60.00

		S	M	L		
410	Midnight Navy/Varsity Red/Midnight Navy/White 2/25					
455	Alpine Blue/Varsity Red/White/Midnight Navy 2/25					

98 FALL 1998 WOMEN'S **SOCCER**

FIG 137

FIG 138

96

FIG 139

FIG 140

FIG 141

FIG 142

This evolution toward women-first design can be traced through the Nike catalogs of the mid-1990s too, where, alongside generic training tanks, team sports–specific jerseys began to find their place for the general consumer. In spring 1994, women's apparel had been designated for aerobics, running, cross-training, tennis, swimwear, and cycling. The jersey appeared under the guise of a running singlet, or something close to it—often in mesh, often with matching shorts. But the needs of a runner are different from those of a football or basketball player. A runner's motion is linear and almost always forward-facing, for starters, and so a singlet requires ease and for air to be able to move in and out of it. Football players, on the other hand, can still cover up to 6.2 miles in any given match, but their game comprises many different motions, and so coverage plays a more important part on the field than on the track.

In the spring 1996 Nike catalog, women's football-specific apparel finally found its place. Pared-back graphics and classic colorways were the main focus, alongside a subtle US women's national football jersey, which featured a simple crew neck, a small swoosh, and a team sports label at the lower left front hem. The shirt was available in navy blue, royal blue, white, and red. By 1997 it seemed women's football had gained the traction it needed to appeal to a general consumer: Nike sold a women's team jersey with the US national football emblem front and center.

The beauty of the team jersey is that while it originated for the professional player on the field, court, or other arena, its life did not end there. With its heavy symbolism and homage to the individual, team, or place, the jersey was ripe to be metabolized by the music industry. Look to the 1990s and early 2000s when Missy Elliott was rarely seen without one. Mariah Carey famously wore Michael Jordan jerseys repurposed as bodycon dresses to perform during the NBA All-Star Game in 2003. (YouTube clips of the moment claim Jordan "almost cried" as the star sang "Hero"[5]—but the jury is out on whether that had more to do with the song or the look.)

Sports jerseys are eaten up by music, but they're chewed up and spat back out again—albeit with love—by fashion. The likes of Ralph Lauren, Celine, Louis Vuitton, and Missoni have all interpreted their iconography many times over many seasons—numbers, stripes, and technical fabrics often playing their part in the designs. Under Francesco Risso's eye at Marni, a retro basketball jersey was sewn up along the bottom hem and repurposed as a tote bag, the armholes doubling as handles. Martine Rose went full circle: street, sports, and subculture have placed jerseys in her line of sight many times since she founded her eponymous label in

FIG 143

FIG 144

2007, so ripe are they for representing a moment or a point of view within a recognized and well-loved lexicon. In 2021 Rose joined forces with Nike to launch a special-edition England supporter's shirt for the Lost Lionesses. It was inspired by the unofficial England women's team that played in the 1971 World Cup, refusing to be suppressed by the English Football Association's fifty-year ban on women's football. (In a perfect tribute, the athlete label reads: "Engineered to the exact specifications of Martine Rose.") More recently, Heaven by Marc Jacobs partnered with Barragán to make a referee minidress, which—with its grass green and red colorway, striped cutaway collar, and cutouts at the upper arms and décolletage—is among the cheekier tributes: the tiny football player pictured in silhouette at the shoulder has their trousers pulled down to their ankles.

The women's jersey was created for women athletes, but the past thirty years have proven that its place is, in fact, everywhere. In the mid-1990s, when female football and basketball players found themselves putting down roots in our collective cultural memory, their rise in popularity took everybody by surprise—the athletes themselves, the companies that clothed and equipped them, even the leagues that granted them an official time and place to play. Individual stars emerged based on their own excellence on the field or the court.

Now, after three decades of concerted effort in continuing to build that heritage, women's team sports are for everybody. Case in point: in 2015 Nike faced a backlash when fans were unable to buy the US women's football jersey in men's sizes. Men wanted to wear the names of their favorite female players, and the two stars above the US Soccer Federation crest that represented the team's World Cup wins in 1991 and 1999. (For men, a women's XL was insufficient.) Nike took note; it began manufacturing the team jerseys in men's sizes. The moment marked another small, but not insignificant, shift in what has become a landslide.

The hallmark moments are real, and they're happening in real time; we are all witnessing them together. As a company of sports fans, Nike's role is not to manufacture those moments but to respond to them; it watches the culture gathering speed and clears the way however it can.

—— 1 ——
Ann Killion, "'Summer of the Women': How 1996 Olympics changed sports forever," July 29, 2016, *San Francisco Chronicle*, www.sfchronicle.com/news/article/Summer-of-the-Women-How-1996-Olympics-8636042.

—— 2 ——
Sally Jenkins, "History of Women's Basketball," WNBA, www.wnba.com/news/history-of-womens-basketball.

—— 3 ——
"The Story of Women's Football in England," The FA, www.thefa.com/womens-girls-football/heritage/kicking-down-barriers.

—— 4 ——
Vanessa Friedman, "Women Finally Get Their Own World Cup Soccer Style," March 11, 2019, *New York Times*, www.nytimes.com/2019/03/11/style/womens-world-cup-kit-nike

—— 5 ——
TwoThreeForever, "Mariah Carey Performs Hero, MJ (Age 39) Almost Cries @ 2003 All-Star Half-Time Break," February 2, 2013, www.youtube.com/watch?v=uGtB8BvPkN0.

FIG 145

FIG 147

FIG 146

FIG 148

FIG 149

FIG 150

FIG 151

dear méxico,

white	varsity red	royal	team red
columbia blue	deep forest	college orange	midnight navy

FIG 152

150 Soccer feature in Women's Apparel Catalog, Spring 2001

151 Mexico Women's Soccer "Dear México," 2001

152 Color Palette, Holiday 2001

153

FIG 153

FIG 154

▼

Mariah Carey famously wore Michael Jordan jerseys repurposed as bodycon dresses to perform during the NBA All-Star Game in 2003—including this one, designed by Reuben Harley, featuring Jordan's signature number twenty-three, to commemorate the athlete's final year in the league.

153 Singer Mariah Carey performs at the 2003 NBA All-Star game in Atlanta

154 Park SZ5 Jersey and Park SZ5 Short, United Jersey and United Short, and SZ5 National Jersey and SZ5 National Short, Spring 2005

FIG 155

155 Australia 2000 Sydney Olympics Women's Basketball Uniform, 2000

156 China 2016 Rio Olympics Vapor Basketball Jersey Worn by Shao Ting, 2016

157 China 2016 Rio Olympics Basketball Shorts, 2016

FIG 156

FIG 157

SPORT TRAINING

SU
08

FIG 159

FIG 160

FIG 161

161

161

162

FIG 162

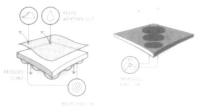

FIG 163

FIG 164

FIG 166

FIG 165

FIG 167

167

333059   **NIKE WOMEN'S WARRIOR JERSEY**   W0521 $25.00

FABRIC

DELIVERY WINDOW

400

070

100

FIG 168

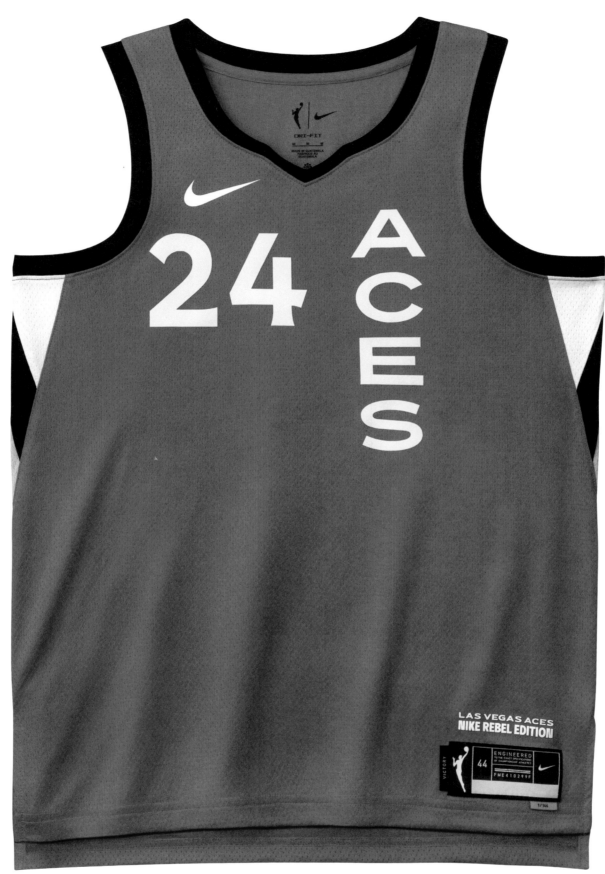

FIG 169

FIG 170

Nike first released WNBA jerseys in 2018, with an armhole created specifically for the female player, providing more comfort and ease of movement than the men's cut had. It marked an exciting moment for the game—new designs created for a new generation of stars and a swathe of new fans across the league. In 2021, the design of game jerseys was modified to introduce a series of three necklines to choose from: a round neck, a V-neck, and the wishbone neckline exclusive to the WNBA.

169 WNBA Jersey Las Vegas, Summer 2024

170 WNBA Jersey Chicago, Summer 2024

FIG **171**

FIG **172**

171 NBA Earned Editions Swooshes, 2018

172 Portland Thorns logo

173 Nike x MadeMe USWNT Jersey, 2019

FIG 173

FIG 174

174

FIG 177

174

174

FIG 175

FIG 176

FIG 178

FIG 179

174 Australia National Team Kit worn by Sam Kerr, 2019

175 Minnesota Timberwolves NBA City Edition Jersey, 2019

176 Los Angeles Lakers NBA City Edition Jersey, 2019

177 Swoosh Fly Reversible Basketball Jersey

178 China National Team Kit, 2019

179 Nike x Marine Serre Bodysuit and Jersey, 2019

FIG 180

FIG 181

FIG 182

FIG 183

FIG 184

185

FIG 185

FIG 186

FIG 187

FIG 188

185 Aori Nishimura during the Women's Street Final, Tokyo 2020 Olympics, 2021

186 Danny Supa FC Jersey, 2001

187 Nike SB USA Skateboarding Federation Tank, 2024

188 Nike SB USA Skateboarding Federation Jersey, 2024

FIG 189

In the summer of 2023, Nike launched a collection in collaboration with Ambush designer Yoon Ahn, which explored football fandom through the jersey. The campaign was shot in its most natural habitat—the locker room.

189 Nike x Ambush Jersey, 2023

FIG 190

FIG 191

190 Skylar Diggins-Smith #4 of the Phoenix Mercury, July 22, 2022

191 USA Basketball Kit worn by Sue Bird and Diana Taurasi, 2020

June 28, 2019. Paris, France.

Megan Rapinoe celebrates in now-iconic fashion after scoring her team's first goal during the 2019 World Cup quarter-final between France and USA.

September 21, 2018. Tenerife, Spain.

Where once she played in the kit, now she coaches in it. Dawn Staley checks in with the USA women's basketball team during practice.

July 26, 2021. Tokyo, Japan.

Rayssa Leal wears her national jersey to compete in the women's street skateboarding finals at the 2020 Summer Olympics.

ATHLETE: **MEGAN RAPINOE**

SUBJECT: **COLLECTING JERSEYS**

BIOGRAPHY: Megan Rapinoe is an American football player. She
was born in 1985 in California, USA.

I have all the jerseys from the most meaningful points in my career, but I also collected a lot from different players over the years.

They are such beautiful markers,

whether we won the game or lost the game.

For the World Cup in 2019, I think I have a jersey from almost every team.

Those are really special, because, oh my God, my whole life changed in a completely and very unexpected way.

To mark that moment, especially in a final, with another player from the opposing team's jersey—

it's the opposite of a trophy of war, in a sense.

It's like, we were in this together.

There is a solidarity in women's sports, and I felt it particularly strongly during that World Cup.

All the teams were a part of something incredible.

It's become a marker for our sport:

before France, and after France.

The whole world was changing around us, because of us.

We were a part of a movement.

ATHLETE: DAWN STALEY

SUBJECT: THE USA JERSEY

BIOGRAPHY: Dawn Staley is an American basketball player and coach. She was born in 1970 in Pennsylvania, USA.

The USA jersey was always too big for me.

It never fit.

That's a uniform that I had a hard time fixing.

I didn't mind my shorts being big—I liked my shorts to hit at my knee, so you're not looking at my knock-knees,

you're just looking at my play—

but the jersey being too big created something else.

And I was a tucker. I tucked my jersey into my tights.

I didn't like it to come out.

When I am in the game, I want everything right. It's got to look right.

It's got to feel right.

ATHLETE: RAYSSA LEAL

SUBJECT: UNIFORM

BIOGRAPHY: Rayssa Leal is a Brazilian skateboarder. She was
born in 2008 in Maranhão, Brazil.

Uniform has always reminded me of, and connected me to, football.

When I was young, I would never have thought skate would have a uniform.

We Brazilians are extremely proud of our colors,

we represent our country anywhere we go.

So it was an incredible experience to wear the Brazilian flag on my chest in Tokyo—

a feeling I will never forget.

ATHLETE: SCOUT BASSETT

SUBJECT: DRESSING AS ACTIVISM

BIOGRAPHY: Scout Bassett is an American track and field athlete who competes in the
100-, 200-, 400- meter sprints, and the long jump, in the T42 classification.
She was born in 1988 in Nanjing, China.

How you look can be a form of activism.

It doesn't have to be crazy loud or obvious,

but I can't tell you how many people I've met when I've been traveling the world doing what I get to do who say, 'Wow.'

Since the beginning of time, people with disabilities in all different forms

have been told that they're unattractive, they're undesirable, that they can't have a disability and be pretty,

or be fit,

or be any of these other things.

They've been told to hide themselves, and to live in shame or guilt.

Clothes can really tell a different story, and that is so powerful.

So the way I show up to work every day is very important to me.

I want everybody I'm training with to see that.

fit

check

samantha n. sheppard

A fit check describes the process of highlighting one's outfit in a series of selfies and posts made on social media sites. Often, though not exclusively, done by young girls and women, this exercise makes public something originally done privately in front of a mirror. What was once a moment of interiority and self-regard becomes a public act and digital performance. Inwardly and outwardly "feeling oneself," this mindset and mode are mediated, a way to mark technological space with one's own signature style. According to fashion historian Carol Tulloch, style is "the construction of self through the assemblage of garments, accessories, and beauty regimes that may, or may not, be 'in fashion' at the time of use."[1] Whether on trend or a throwback, color-coordinated or a disruption of decorum, fit checks are about how we style our bodies and design our lives with and through clothing. As a fashion system, these assessments break down the sum of one's outfit into its elemental parts. It's about serving looks and structuring looking relations: peep the thrifted shirt, the name-brand shoes, the icy jewelry. Categories of dress and designer are captured through oscillating full-body and close-up imagery that balances viewers' desires for individual details and ensemble cohesion. Sometimes chic, sometimes tacky, always for public consumption and critique. These modes of self-fashioning articulate personal "style narratives."[2] In short, fit checks are about who we are, what we wear, and why it matters.

What might it mean to embrace this mode of everyday sartorial splendor to assess sportswear? Designed to be seen both close-up and at a distance, in a stadium and on screens, sportswear embellishes and enhances the play and persona of the sporting self(ie). This is true for both men and women—but while there are countless examples of male athletes' style and sporting moments, what of women athletes specifically? How do women's sportswear choices affect their athletic performances? Given the history of women's marginalization in sports, fit checks of women's sportswear articulate an aesthetic of presence in arenas long thought to be the domain of men. Stylization, in this sense, points to the agency women athletes have in producing their own looks within and through sportswear's staid structures. Of significance here are the modifying and accessorizing of standard professional athletic attire by women athletes. Choices in hair color and texture, cutouts in body stockings, defiance in all black, or a riot of color enhance and advance critical and popular discourses on women's sports, beauty, pleasure, and celebrity.

The fit checks I examine here capture moments of delight and controversy within the contemporary history of women's competitive tennis, track and field, and soccer: the excesses exalted by Florence "Flo-Jo" Griffith Joyner's plum one-legger; the conventions smashed by Serena Williams's (super)powerful black catsuit; the provocation (counter)posed by Megan Rapinoe's outstanding uniformity; and the defiant growth revealed by Sha'Carri Richardson's changing coiffure.

— 1 —
Carol Tulloch, *The Birth of Cool: Style Narratives of the African Diaspora* (New York: Bloomsbury Visual Arts, 2016), 4.

— 2 —
Tulloch, 5.

She served looks, muscle, and magic all at once.

Signature looks become a part of the game and its wider discourse, shaping performance, fandom, and fashion in evocative ways. Perhaps no other sport has as rich a history of self-fashioning as track and field, with many of its most memorable sartorial spectacles worn by one of its greatest athletes. Florence "Flo-Jo" Griffith Joyner's eye-catching looks and signature style stitched together color as palette and as race, inducing visceral emotions and commentary while shattering expectations and world records. Griffith Joyner contravened the blandness of track uniforms through innovative redesigns of traditional leotards and bodysuits. She also used nails, jewelry, makeup, and hair to produce what academic Jillian Hernandez calls an "aesthetic of excess," pointing to "diasporic iconographies and practices of bodily styling, art making, and cultural production" specific to Black women that use clothing and accessories to embellish and critique broader notions of play, pleasure, and personhood.[3]

Her style, bold and vibrant, matched the exceptionality of her 100-meter world-record-setting 10.49-second sprint at the quarterfinals of the US Olympic Trials in 1988. During that race she wore a now-well-known one-legged plum-colored leotard with a polka-dotted and zigzag-patterned turquoise bikini brief. With jet-black hair flowing, glam makeup popping, and six-inch-long orange manicured nails pumping, Griffith Joyner electrified the track with her conspicuous embodiment and searing speed. Her fashionable one-legger is exquisitely excessive, enhancing the "sports star/Barbie doll" spectacle of her athletic feats. Indeed, a version of this asymmetrical running suit would become the basis for the Flo-Jo doll released the following year. The revealing tailoring, bold color choices, and contrasting patterns are in keeping with Griffith Joyner's sports and fashion experimentation that began at her Los Angeles public high school, where she convinced her teammates to wear long tights with their uniforms. Later in her professional career, she donned various spandex bodysuits and two-pieces to enhance her sporting performance. After retirement, Griffith Joyner continued her work as a fashion designer, including designing the uniforms worn by the Indiana Pacers from 1990 to 1997.

Griffith Joyner's eye-catching looks flaunted hyperfeminine aesthetics to dazzle audiences, signaling a "desire to utilize the body creatively, admire one's self-image, and potentially attract the gazes of others."[4] Griffith Joyner famously expressed: "Dress good to look good. Look good to feel good. And feel good to run fast!" If sporting and social identities and excellence are stitched together via sportswear, Griffith Joyner's glam fit constructed and critiqued narratives about herself, women athletes, and Black women. Her flamboyant style now serves as a reminder and rebuttal of track and field's social history. As sports historian Susan Cahn explains, "The assertion that

---

[3] Jillian Hernandez, *Aesthetics of Excess: The Art and Politics of Black and Latina Embodiment* (Durham, NC: Duke University Press, 2020), 10.

---

[4] Hernandez., 11.

"I feel like a warrior in it,

a warrior princess . . ."

sport made women physically unattractive and sexually unappealing found its corollary in views of Black women as less attractive and desirable than white women."[5] Griffith Joyner's plum one-legger blended feminine appeal with sporting dominance. With it, she served looks, muscle, and magic all at once.

FIT CHECK:
SERENA WILLIAMS'S
(SUPER)POWERFUL BLACK CATSUIT

One might assume that women's athletic uniforms meant to promote a brand, team, and/or national affiliation construct singular narratives about sportswear and individual sporting figures. However, fit checks can reveal the complex ways athletes flaunt their individual style against and through the hegemony of their sport's uniformity. This is acutely the case when one considers the world of tennis, which historically maintained strict racialized codes and sporting norms that discouraged difference and diversity. That was until the Williams sisters came onto the court. "From the beginning of their careers," Nicole Fleetwood explains, "Venus and Serena moved away from the conventions of tennis fashion and incorporated bolder colors, a variety of fabrics and patterns, and urban and Black accessories."[6] Through both her participation and dominance, Serena Williams transformed the narrow ideals associated with the sport in a dramatic and contentious public fashion. While there is a panoply of Serena's on-court styles worthy of fit checks, her black full-body catsuit at the 2018 French Open is an iconic design and sports-historic moment worthy of detailed analysis.

The sleek full-length Nike bodysuit with a vibrant red waistband was not conventional tennis attire. Punctuated with shimmering silver-and-black Nike tennis shoes, Williams looked both regal and ready to play, with her hair pulled tightly into a bun at the top of her head. The look marked Williams's return to the French Open after giving birth to her first child. For the tennis GOAT, the look had personal and performative functions. She explained to reporters: "I feel like a warrior in it, a warrior princess . . . from Wakanda, maybe," referencing the blockbuster Black superhero film *Black Panther* (directed by Ryan Coogler, 2018). Williams continued: "I've always wanted to be a superhero, and it's kind of my way of being a superhero." The outfit's heroic dimension included its health-conscious design; the skin-tight leggings of the catsuit provided compression therapy, an element needed to assist her blood circulation as Williams developed pulmonary blood clots after the birth of her daughter.

French Tennis Federation president Bernard Giudicelli slammed her outfit, saying it had "gone too far." The suit's simple but (super)powerful design and the insipid response by protocol-setting opponents is in keeping with the history of racial transgressions that Serena symbolized and

5

Susan Cahn, *Coming on Strong: Gender and Sexuality in Twentieth-Century Women's Sport* (Cambridge, MA: Harvard University Press, 1994), 127–8.

6

Nicole Fleetwood, *On Racial Icons: Blackness and the Public Imagination* (New Brunswick, NJ: Rutgers University Press, 2015), 100.

materialized when she played. Giudicelli's clichéd critique highlights the history of how Serena and her sister Venus were "cast as anomalous to the sport—not quite right/not quite white for women's tennis."[7] In a defiant turn, Serena's fashion choices often altered expectations and set new standards for women's tennis, and Black women in sports in general. The image of Williams in her catsuit at her first Grand Slam after becoming a mother circulated in ways that empowered fans as she smashed conventions, which she did during her entire unprecedented career that includes thirty-nine major titles, twenty-three Grand Slams, four Olympic medals, and 319 weeks ranked as world number one by the Women's Tennis Association.

FIT CHECK: MEGAN RAPINOE'S OUTSTANDING UNIFORMITY

Uniforms link teammates on the field into a collective chromatic and stylistic mass. Take, for example, the US Women's National Team's (USWNT) "home" uniforms for the 2019 FIFA Women's World Cup in France. The Nike-designed all-white uniform featured a jersey with red and blue bands on the sleeves, signaling cuffs worn by former celebrated '99ers Brandi Chastain, Mia Hamm, and Julie Foudy. Above the team crest rested three stars, representing the three times that the United States had won the world title—1991, 1999, and 2015—a motif repeated at the nape of the neck, on the back of the jersey, and on the shorts. The jersey's back panel shifted from white to a tonal gray used to print the names of all fifty states, and just inside the collar, where the tag would usually reside, it read: ONE NATION. ONE TEAM. Team uniforms are "about individual image and group regard."[8] Each individual part is meant to magnify the whole look of the team as connected to each other and the American people, turning sportswear into emblematic designs of national identity and belonging. They produce and inform social identities and speak to broader cultural narratives. In this manner, women's sportswear is multitextured and multivalent.

Individual players, however, disrupt uniformity and anonymity by tailoring individual and collective values and cultural politics into their sportswear. These details set them apart as well as connect them to other fields of play. The most widespread image from the 2019 FIFA Women's World Cup is that of Megan Rapinoe's post-goal celebration pose during the quarterfinals against France. The image shows Rapinoe running to the corner after netting the first goal in the match, her arms outstretched, a sly smile on her face, which is flanked by her purple hair as she faces the stadium filled with cheering fans. It is now perhaps one of the most recognizable images from women's soccer history, period. (Chastain's spontaneous post–penalty kick Nike bra reveal is another.) With her teammates trailing behind to embrace her, Rapinoe for a moment stood

Rapinoe's uniform, posture, smirk, and hair form a queer, critical gesture and stylistic counterpose.

— 7 —

Samantha N. Sheppard, *Sporting Blackness: Race, Embodiment, and Critical Muscle Memory on Screen* (Oakland, CA: University of California Press, 2020), 3.

— 8 —

Monica L. Miller, *Slaves to Fashion: Black Dandyism and the Styling of Black Diasporic Identity* (Durham, NC: Duke University Press, 2009), 3.

out from the team's monochromatic mass and articulated a different embodied message.

Rapinoe defies her team uniform's monological signaling of nationhood, US patriotism, and normative sporting and social categories (white, male, heterosexual, etc.). Her queer sporting body highlights the underheralded and historically unarticulated position of lesbians in women's sports and society. The homophobic violence and historical erasure that constitute American patriarchal patriotism are challenged by Rapinoe's publicly queer identification and celebration, which is embraced by her teammates and fans. She alters the fabric of unity/uniformity by dressing down authoritative aesthetics and agents. As ESPN sportswriter Caitlin Murray explains, Rapinoe's look and gesture "showed both confidence and vulnerability, defiance and affection all at the same time. It was an expression of joy but also a clapback to Donald Trump and his supporters, who rooted against Rapinoe and the USWNT when she made clear during an interview that she would decline any invitation to the White House if the US won the World Cup."[9] In the celebratory moment in the aforementioned photograph, Rapinoe's uniform, posture, smirk, and hair form a queer, critical gesture and stylistic counterpose. These design counternarratives speak to and move against what it might mean to be "one nation, one team." Her activism and outspoken history on civil rights fashion a freedom not guaranteed by patriotism or team collectivism. Rather, transgression, multiplicity, and differentiation are her way of standing out and being outstanding among her team.

FIT CHECK:
SHA'CARRI RICHARDSON'S
CHANGING COIFFURE

Sha'Carri Richardson's sporting style infuses a similar maximalist approach to that of the legend Florence Griffith Joyner. But while Richardson's track outfits lack the kind of sartorial novelty of the former world record holder, her overall sporting ensemble—particularly her changing hairstyles and hair color—draws from the same Black vernacular traditions. The iconic image of Richardson during the 100-meter final of the 2023 USA Track and Field Outdoor Championships captures a moment of dramatic transformation. As Richardson waits at the starting blocks alongside her competitors for her name to be announced, she looks ready to prove all of her doubters wrong. Wearing a Nike green and teal, patterned short-legged leotard with a plunging neckline that highlights the tattoos on her arms and sternum, she sways side to side in anticipation of the final race. Her fiery orange hair—pulled back in a low ponytail and away from her face with a green headband with a pink Nike swoosh—creates contrast between her and the rest of the athletes, who wear slight variations of the shared branded uniform style. Richardson at first appears unbothered by the stalking camera as the stadium announcer declares her name and lane. However, she quickly removes her hair and headband to reveal an intricately cornrowed braid design with blonde highlights flowing down her back. Staring directly into the camera, her new look and pointed gaze signify that she is ready to get down to business. And she did, as Richardson clinched her first national title with a time of 10.84 seconds.

In an interview following the win, Richardson explained: "The reason why I did the wig reveal, I had my orange hair last time. I wanted to show I'm still that girl but I'm better, stronger, and wiser. I had to shed the old and present the new." Richardson's decisive act both attaches and detaches her hair and sense of self to her previous performance at the 2020 US Olympic Trials, where she won the 100-meter race and qualified for the Tokyo Olympics. During the trials, long, flame-colored tresses flowed from her head as she smoked her competitors. The half-up hairdo included two curl tendrils framing her jubilant face. Her spectacular styling extended to her long ombre coral acrylic nails, gold bracelets and necklace, impossibly long eyelashes, and two nose studs. Unapologetically herself, her fiery hair and spirit were captured in post-heats where she admonished her haters, "Stop playing with me" and proudly proclaimed, "I'm that girl," to the world.

Ultimately, Richardson was banned from the 2020 Olympic Games in Tokyo for testing positive for marijuana, and she quickly lost popular support. She was both penalized and vilified for the indiscretion despite explaining that she used marijuana medicinally to deal with the pain of her biological mother's death. Richardson's 2023 wig reveal was a reclamation, a sign of both growth and acceptance. It was not a capitulation to the critiques that circulated about her in 2020 but a critical commentary upon them: "I'm still that girl, but I'm better. I'm still that girl, but I'm stronger. I'm still that girl, but I'm wiser." To think about hair as an extension of sportswear (either put on or removed before the starter's gun) is to recognize that the image of Richardson's plaits represents coiled identities, liberating tangles, and textures of an evolving sporting self.

9 Caitlin Murray, "Megan Rapinoe's Top 10 Most Memorable USWNT Moments," ESPN, September 20, 2023, www.espn.com/soccer/story/_/id/38418343/megan-rapinoe-most-memorable-uswnt-moments-top-ten.

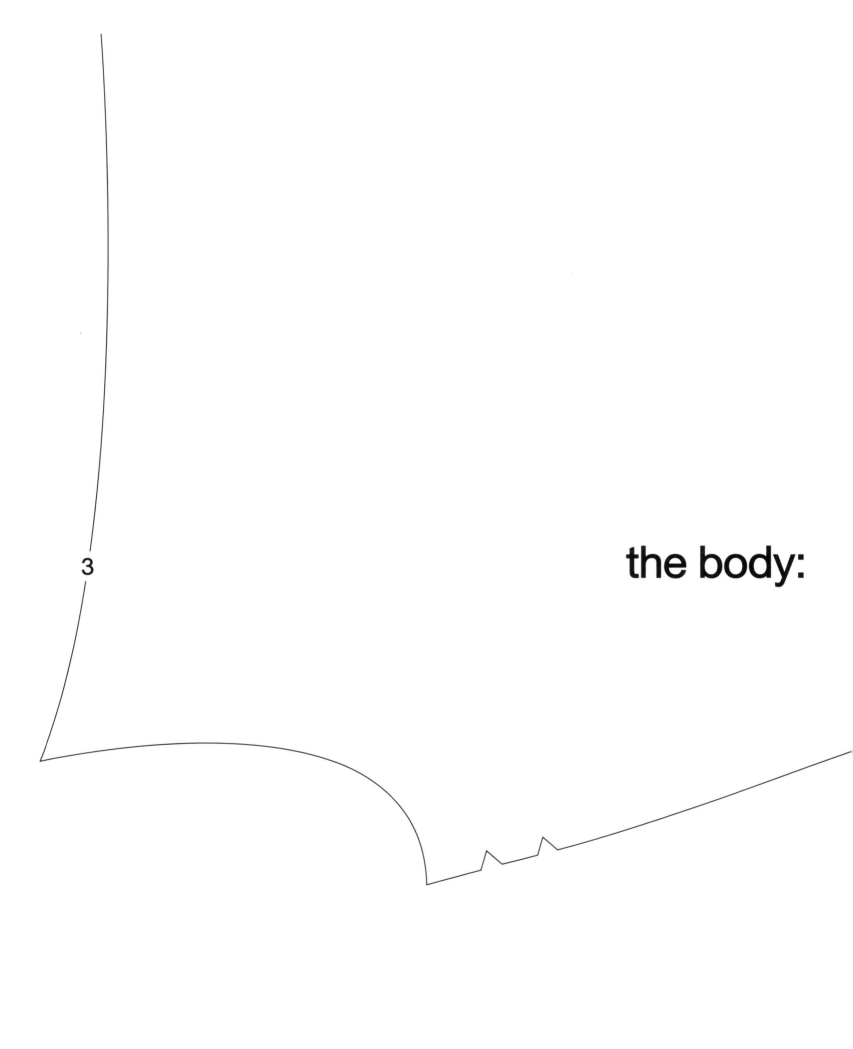

the body:

3

seen

Many on the street were not used to see

ng so much body, from so many bodies.

148

leggings

FIG 192

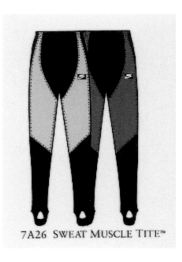

7A26 SWEAT MUSCLE TITE™

FIG 193

192 Sweat Muscle Tite, Fall 1986

193 Sportswear, 1984

194 Interval Singlet and Muscle Tite Two-Color Tight, Fall 1985

195 Color Block Shortsleeve and Sweat Muscle Tite, Fall 1986

Leggings are tight-fitting pants made from a lightweight, stretchy fabric, usually a blend of nylon, polyester, and spandex. To wear them is to feel comfortable, supported, streamlined. You know this, most likely. If you don't wear them yourself, you see them every day: On a treadmill in the gym. Stopping in quickly at the grocery store, sweater sleeves knotted loosely around the waist. Waiting in line at the coffee shop. Jogging laps at the local park, an abbreviated selection of house keys and a credit card tucked into a surreptitious pocket at the lower back. This is because leggings are ubiquitous—and they are so because they are extraordinarily good at what they do.

At Nike, leggings were initially developed in the early 1980s for men to wear while running. (They were called *tights* to begin with, a marketing decision made to create distance from the fashion garment that had dominated womenswear in the late 1960s and 1970s. For Nike women's apparel, the name was changed back to leggings relatively recently.) It's difficult to imagine—rarely had the world seen bodycon clothing on men outside of the swimming pool in that era. But when American track-and-field athlete Carl Lewis peeled off the Muscle Tite tights in a vivid black-and-orange colorway before competing in the Olympic trials ahead of the 1984 Games in Los Angeles—where he'd go on to win four gold medals, becoming one of the greatest athletes of the century—he made an excellent case for them. The popular product was launched to customers, both male and female, in the spring catalog the following year.

From an athletic point of view, the appeal was simple: leggings provided a warm, light layer that was easy to move in. They were designed to wick sweat away from the skin, were comfortable (even for long periods), and were easy to layer—particularly when it came to skiing and other outdoor sports that required bulky or protective clothing. They'd been around for several centuries, in fact, as a form of undergarment often paired with armor, before they were adopted as everyday apparel in the 1960s and as sportswear soon afterward.

Aesthetically, however, their swift and widespread rise to popularity in the 1980s—among professionals and amateurs, men and women, the short and tall, slim and stocky—caused a stir. Many on the street were not used to seeing so much body from so many bodies. "You can see them jogging any morning on San Vicente Boulevard's grassy strip: young, lean, physically fit paragons of yuppiness," wrote Bettijane Levine for the *Los Angeles Times* in January 1985. "From the waist up, there's nothing new to notice. From the waist

FIG 194

FIG 195

down, they're the next best thing to nude. They're wearing running tights—the hottest new item in sports apparel—an item commercially available for less than a year, but now selling by leaps and bounds."[1]

The stretchy, form-fitting properties of leggings are made possible by spandex, or elastane, a synthetic fabric invented by DuPont chemist Joseph Shivers in the early 1950s. It was created in a bid to replace rubber—a hot, heavy material, often used in girdles and other restrictive undergarments, that broke down on exposure to oils, perspiration, lotions, and detergents.[2] The result was patented as Lycra in 1962, and once blended with fibers such as cotton, wool, silk, and linen, it was both lighter in weight than rubber and more wear-resistant. As hoped, Lycra was quickly adopted for use in underwear and was incorporated into swimwear and other clothes soon afterward.[3]

In the pool, spandex's form-fitting properties—clinging to and outlining every muscle, angle, and curve—felt familiar, even reasonable. It allowed swimmers to move through the water with as little obstruction as possible. Likewise, away from the pool, spandex was considered acceptable attire in professional athletic competition; it was worn by elite sportspeople in prime physical condition, after all, and at a respectable distance from quotidian apparel. But when leggings hit the street, donned by amateur athletes of all shapes and sizes, people began to take notice. "The tights are being worn by both sexes," Levine continued, "with nothing over them to cover the lower torso, fore, or aft."[4] The exposure of the physical form in such clarity, and with such regularity, was a revelation. Bodycon sportswear had truly arrived.

The initial meaning of *bodycon* is difficult to pinpoint—it might derive from *body-contouring, body-conscious*, or *body-conforming*. Since the term's arrival in our lexicon sometime in the late twentieth century, its definition has remained ambiguous; at times it refers to a body shaped by clothing (not unlike the rubber girdles Shivers sought to upgrade), and at other times it applies to clothing that is shaped by the body. Bodycon's impact in apparel for women is similarly ambiguous, oscillating between empowerment and objectification in a space in which neither extreme is entirely divisible from the other. For example, a woman might dress in tight-fitting clothing that displays the body rather than disguises it, and discover the power of shedding shame around her physicality. Or perhaps she internalizes society's pervasive narratives about what that body should look like and aspires to alter its shape, working to make it bigger, rounder, smaller, firmer.

FIG 197

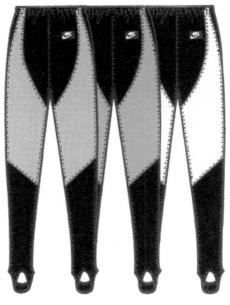

FIG 198

FIG 196

7AV1   Cross-Training Swimtard

FIG 201

FIG 199

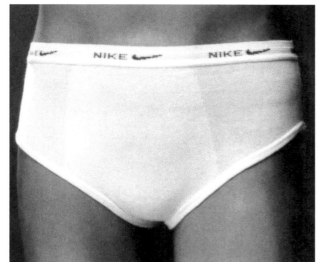

FIG 200

▼

With a high waist and a cropped leg, Audrey Hepburn's capri pants were an elegant predecessor to the leggings of the 1960s. This photograph, taken as part of the publicity campaign surrounding the 1954 movie *Sabrina*, captures her character's Parisian style with a muted color palette and a bold line—and paved the way for tighter fits to follow.

196 Page from Women's Apparel Catalog, Spring 1985

197 Color Palette, Fall 1985

198 Muscle-Tite Two Color, Fall 1986

199 Sport Brief, Spring 1983

200 Audrey Hepburn in a publicity photo to promote the movie *Sabrina*, 1954

201 Page from Cross-Training Collection Catalog, Fall 1990

202 Lite Tite, Fall 1986

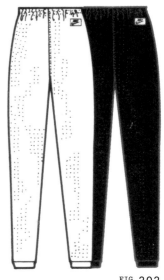

FIG 202

RUN AROUND NAKED. KINDA.

The ultra-light tights feel fast. The feather-weight jacket feels fast. The *very* light shoe feels *very* fast. It's the Nike Air Flow. With a Phylon™ midsole, a dynamic stretch nylon forefoot. And Nike-Air. Normally, when something feels this good, you hope nobody's watching.

Featured apparel: Chevron Tight; Chevron Jacket.

Air Flow

FIG 203

154

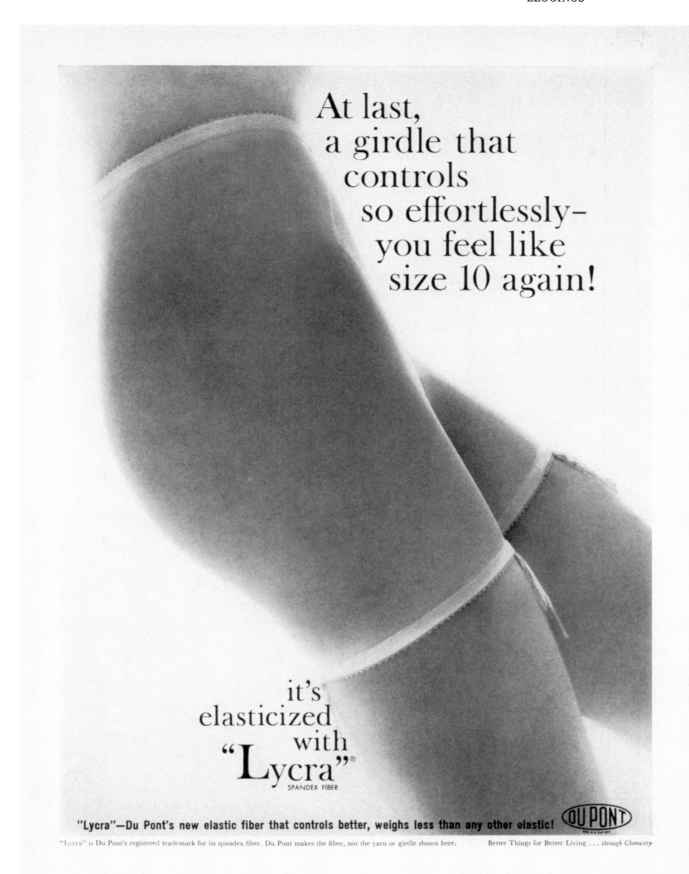

FIG 204

203 Air Flow, Chevron Full Zip Jacket and Chevron Tight in "Run Around
    Naked. Kinda" featuring Mark Allen, 1988

204 DuPont Lycra ad depicting the mid-section of a woman modeling a girdle,
    c. 1960

Or she receives unwanted attention—is objectified, diminished, sexualized. For women of color, women who are large, and women with disabilities, the impact is even more insidious.

And yet, bodycon—and leggings—can feel so good. Support without restriction. Warmth, comfort, ease. Leggings for sports at Nike originated with running in the 1980s—at a time when a super slim body type was the "ideal" for many wearers—and they were quickly adopted across disciplines: for dance, training, studio fitness, yoga, and as a base layer for team sports. Before long, their practical and aesthetic appeal saw them crop up in almost all sporting spaces, and domestic ones too—either for comfort or practicality, donned for traveling to and from a workout. Their astounding popularity precipitated a greater development. By the early 2000s, the tide of body positivity had changed, and society's focus was shifting to strength, irrespective of size. As culture became more inclusive of different types of bodies, leggings were democratized—and as more people wore leggings, the culture became more inclusionary. The trajectory has not always been smooth, but in the athletes of today, you'll find bodies of wildly varying proportions, shapes, and sizes.

Nike is emphatic about its mission statement: "To bring inspiration and innovation to every athlete* in the world." With the all-important qualifying asterisk: "*If you have a body, you are an athlete." As far as leggings are concerned, that means designing them for everybody, and *every body.* Fit, therefore, is crucial. At one time in the company's history, the product team would design a garment for its audience's base size—say, a medium—and then adapt it, scaling up or down for other sizes. The effect was hit and miss; what worked for a small, narrow-hipped body might not be flattering on a full curve, and vice versa.

Nowadays, designers sketch on the full spectrum of sizes from small to 3XL from the very beginning of their process, adapting key elements throughout. The team works with digital software that allows it to scan in more than one hundred thousand morphotypes, or different separations of body mass, within the same size categories. Working with access to such an extensive cross-section of sizes allows designers to understand more fully the dispersion of bodyweight, and to make the very best and most inclusive garments they can.

When it comes to leggings, their challenge is complicated further by the garment's simplicity. Not least because there are so few parts—waistband, legs, gusset, seams, and stitching—meaning the details are incredibly specific. Most important, from the designers' point of view, are fit, material, construction, and style.

FIG 206

FIG 205

1B69 OPTIC TIGHT

1B76 OPTIC SHORT

205 Optic Tight and Optic Short, Fall 1987

206 Cross-Training Apparel Pattern by Amanda Briggs, 1989

207 Page from Women's Apparel Catalog (detail), Fall 1987

208 Page from Women's Apparel Catalog, Fall 1988

156

FIG 207

FIG 208

FIG 209

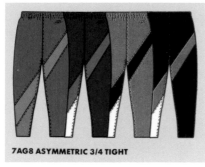

7AG8 ASYMMETRIC 3/4 TIGHT

FIG 210

FIG 211

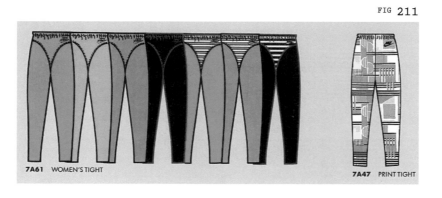

7A61   WOMEN'S TIGHT

7A47   PRINT TIGHT

Or approached from a different angle: How does it fit you? Does it feel good? Does it look good? How about when you move?

With parameters this tight, the demands made upon creativity and innovation are high. Higher still are the baselines of quality set internally for garments such as leggings; as a company rooted in sportswear, Nike's table stakes are far greater than those of competitors that are newer to the leggings market. Take the material, for instance: Nike leggings are held to very high standards for performance, opacity, color, snagging, and tear strength. All Nike leggings are Dri-FIT, meaning they are made using an innovative, high-performance polyester, moisture-wicking fabric that supports the body's natural cooling mechanism. Some include mesh panels, inserted with the guidance of body mapping to allow optimal airflow to high-heat areas. Some include up to six pockets, permitting trail runners and other endurance athletes to carry everything they might need. All are designed to withstand, even excel under, the extreme conditions created during sports.

Style is also important. As trends have shifted over the past forty years, leggings have changed to accommodate them. Picture some of the early inspirations. Dancers pouring out of ballet school in the city, sweaters shrugged on and legwarmers hiked up. Olivia Newton-John stubbing out a cig wearing a high-waisted, high-shine disco pant precursor in *Grease* (1978). Or Blondie frontwoman Debbie Harry in a bright blue, or red-and-gold-striped, or leopard print pair in the late 1970s.

In Nike's trade catalogs, the spandex spirit of leggings resonates through neighboring categories and is irresistible for its campy glitz. As aerobics and studio fitness culture peaked in the late 1980s and early 1990s, Nike upped the ante on shorts, leotards, and unitards across the board. Juxtaposed with the comparative austerity of early 1970s silhouettes and colors, this bright, jazzy, joyful mood had more to do with Wham!'s brash silliness than disco's glamorous swathes, and it presented a profound sense of freedom. Spandex offered up a canvas for play: graphic prints, dynamic shapes, go-faster triangles, and co-ordinated colors. Fashion and sportswear borrowed freely from one another, the fabric a touchpoint in the symbiotic relationship the two fields had long shared.

By the 1990s, leggings at Nike had become to sports apparel what the graphic T-shirt had become to fashion. They served as an excellent vehicle for color and print, and the brand quickly recognized their

FIG 212

209 Page from Women's Apparel Catalog, Spring 1990

210 Asymmetric 3/4 Tight, Fall 1989

211 Women's Tight and Print Tight, Spring 1988

212 Madonna in *Desperately Seeking Susan*, 1985

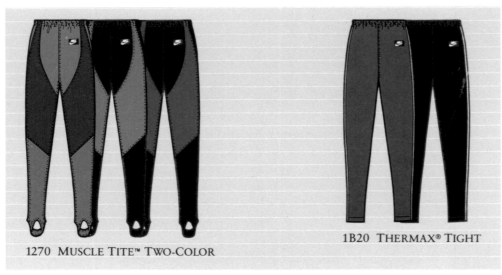

1270 MUSCLE TITE™ TWO-COLOR   1B20 THERMAX® TIGHT

FIG 213

FIG 214

FIG 215

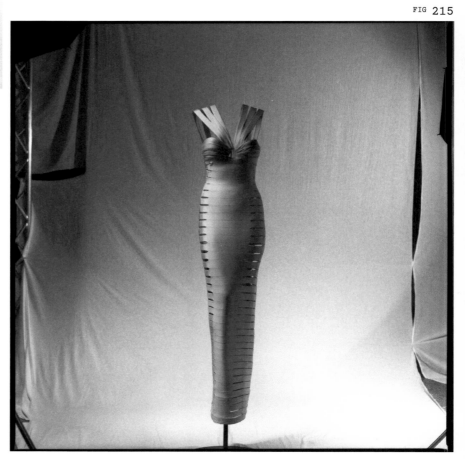

potential to harness what was internally dubbed "the culture of launch." Beginning in 2012, Nike produced limited runs of vibrant designs as part of "Tight of the Moment," a campaign that ran for two or three years. Using digital sublimation, a process in which a heat press sends ink from a printed image onto a piece of fabric, designers were able to place prints with incredible precision, often body-mapping to accentuate an athlete's movements in a flattering way.

In the 2020s wearers tend to be drawn to simpler styles that offer greater versatility and thus a longer lifespan. Personal style is often expressed through muted color palettes, nuanced textures, and changes in rise (low, mid, or high) and leg (from styles that are fitted through the ankle to bootcut and wide leg; leggings have often followed denim trends). Moreover, leggings are one of the product categories that exists far beyond the confines of sports for women. Often leggings signify an active life—a day bookended with a spin or yoga class—or just a busy schedule. But if the sporting goods industry learned anything from the COVID-19 pandemic, it was that Nike customers wanted the comfort, practicality, and ease offered by the company's sportswear across every part of their existence.

Beyond the studio, spandex has always had its space in track-and-field—and not only during warm-ups. In the 2000 Sydney Olympics, indigenous Australian athlete Cathy Freeman achieved icon status, winning gold in the 400-meter final wearing the Swift Suit—a one-piece in gray and teal, referred to over and over again in news coverage as a "spacesuit."[5] Covering the wearer literally from head to toe, the Swift Suit featured a hood for maximum effectiveness against drag and fastened under the heels with stirrups, and it placed different fabrics and textures across different body parts to maximize velocity. Freeman reportedly had reservations about the way she looked in the suit but could not resist the way it felt on her body: "Like you're slicing through the air," she commented in a Nike testing session.

Champion middle-distance runner Caster Semenya's apparel of choice on race day remains a bodysuit, a garment that borrows from the lexicon of leggings with its tightness. On her form, the close-fitting one-piece serves as a reclamation, an affirmation of ownership. The two-time Olympic gold medalist and three-time World Athletics Champion has been subject to invasive questions and testing about her gender identity since she won gold by a stunning margin in the women's 800-meter race at the World Athletics

FIG 216

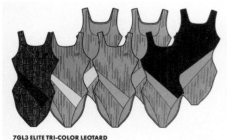

7GL3 ELITE TRI-COLOR LEOTARD

7AJ0 ELITE 3/4 LENGTH RIB TIGHT

Women's Apparel Fall 1989

FIG 217

213 Muscle Tite Two-Color and Thermax Tite, Fall 1987

214 Engraving by Polidor Pauquet, *The Book of Historical Costumes*, Plate V, 1868

215 Long dress with stretch rayon strips, Alaïa, Spring/Summer 1990

216 Elite Tri-color Leotard and Elite 3/4-length Rib Tight, Spring 1989

217 Cover of Women's Apparel Catalog, Fall 1989

FIG 218

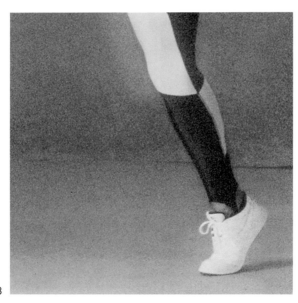

218

218 "The Metallic Group By Nike" sales brochure, 1986

219 Air Trainer SC in "Cross Training is More Aerobic than Aerobics," 1990

WE INTERRUPT THIS AEROBIC WORKOUT TO BRING YOU AN IMPORTANT MESSAGE.

67

FIG 219

FIG 220

FIG 221

FIG 222

220 "Fitness" Poster, 1986

221 Huarache Printed Spandex Tight, 1993

222 International Lycra Tight, 1992

Championships as an eighteen-year-old in 2009. To stand on the starting line in her body was to demand its recognition, its validity, its belonging.

For Freeman and Semenya, as for many professional athletes, fewer, tighter layers mean faster times. But spandex can also possess potentially life-saving properties, particularly for those with pre-existing conditions. When Serena Williams stepped out to play at the 2018 French Open, just eight months after giving birth to her first daughter, she wore a sleek black bodysuit with a poppy red waistband. The one-piece was designed with compressive properties to help prevent the blood clots that had threatened her life after childbirth. Nonetheless, the French Tennis Federation banned the garment, citing a need to "respect the game and the place"[6] in a widely criticized ruling that exemplified the outdated ideas that proliferate around tennis apparel.

In leggings, as in close-fitting clothing more broadly, athletes find style, speed, practicality, and even health benefits. But perhaps a celebration of the body has its part to play too. "Many instructors say they can chart their clients' changing physical confidence by subtle variations in their clothing," Allison Kyle Leopold wrote in the *New York Times*.[7] "When people first start an exercise program, they tend to wear baggy outfits that hide the body," Sean Kelleher, head trainer at Radu, explains. "As they become more comfortable in the gym and get into better shape, they change to more closely fitting clothes, sleeveless tops, and brighter colors."

At the gym, the supermarket, the coffee shop, or the park, leggings present a perfect example of the adage "Look good, feel good, play good," in which "playing good" pertains to the track, the court, and the street. "I went to a disco the other night, and I saw a girl in running tights with a big sweater and boots," New York designer Anita Jacobs told Levine for her 1985 *Los Angeles Times* piece. "She looked wonderful."[8]

—— 1 ——

Bettijane Levine, "TIGHTS: There's Something New in the Running: Running Tights Make Fast Trek to the Top with Fitness Buffs," *Los Angeles Times*, January 25, 1985, www.latimes.com/archives/la-xpm-1985-01-25-vw-9508-story.

—— 2 ——

Kat Eschner, "Thank (?) Joseph Shivers for Spandex," Smithsonian, November 29, 2017, www.smithsonianmag.com/smart-news/thank-joseph-shivers-spandex-180967335.

—— 3 ——

Marc Reisch, "What's That Stuff?" *Chemical and Engineering News*, February 15, 1999, pubsapp.acs.org/cen/whatstuff/stuff/7707scitek4, in Kat Eschner, 2017.

—— 4 ——

Levine, "TIGHTS," 1985.

—— 5 ——

Chris Barrett, "She Won Gold and a Nation's Hearts. This Is How Cathy Freeman's Superset Was Born," *Sydney Morning Herald*, August 14, 2020, www.smh.com.au/sport/she-won-gold-and-a-nation-s-hearts-this-is-how-cathy-freeman-s-supersuit-was-born-20200810-p55k5v.

—— 6 ——

Krystin Arneson, "Nike Has the Perfect Response to That Serena Williams Catsuit Ban," *Glamour*, August 25, 2018, www.glamour.com/story/nike-response-to-serena-williams-catsuit-ban.

—— 7 ——

Allison Kyle Leopold, "Workout Clothes: From the Gym to the Street, a Relaxed Style of Dressing," *New York Times*, September 28, 1986, www.nytimes.com/1986/09/28/magazine/workout-clothes-from-the-gym-to-the-street-a-relaxed-style-of-dressing.

—— 8 ——

Levine, "TIGHTS," 1985.

FIG 223

FIG 224

FIG 225

ROYAL BLUE

TIDAL BLUE

FIG 226

FIG 227

223 International Lycra Tight, Fall 1992

224 Cover of Women's Apparel Catalog (detail), Fall 1990

225 Cross-Trainer Low in "The Body You Have," 1991

226 Color Palette, Spring 1998

227 Page from Women's Apparel Catalog, Spring 1990

FIG 228

228

FIG 229

7BH8 SIGNATURE SHORT

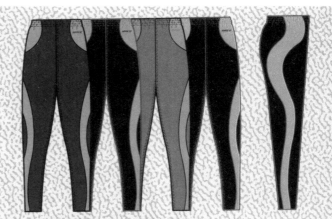

7BJ4 SIGNATURE NYLON/LYCRA® TIGHT

7BH9 SIGNATURE NYLON/LYCRA® SHORT

7BJ6 SIGNATURE UNLINED FULL-ZIP

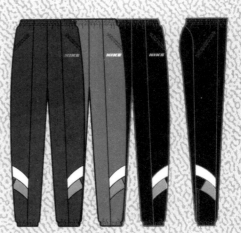

7BJ7 SIGNATURE UNLINED PANT

220137 FITNESS ESSENTIALS MINI

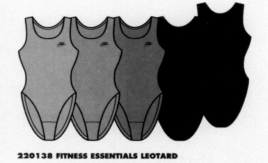

220138 FITNESS ESSENTIALS LEOTARD

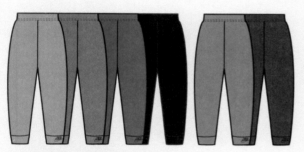

220139 FITNESS ESSENTIALS SHORT

220140 FITNESS ESSENTIALS 3/4 TIGHT

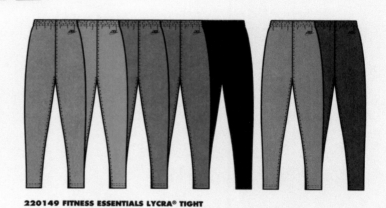

220149 FITNESS ESSENTIALS LYCRA® TIGHT

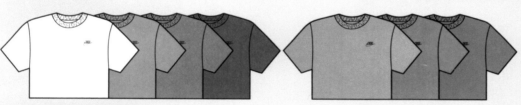

220142 FITNESS ESSENTIALS CROP

FIG 230

FIG 231

FIG 232

232

FIG 233

FIG 234

FIG 235

231 Page from Women's Apparel Catalog, Spring 1993

232 Elite Jazz Fitness Short and Elite Jazz Tight, Fall 1992

233 Essentials feature, Fall 1992

234 Page from Accessories Catalog, Spring 1992

235 Cotton/Lycra Tight and Crop Tee, Fall 1992

FIG 236

FIG 237

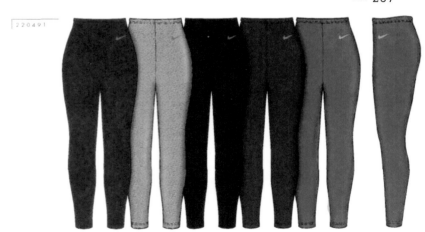

COTTON–SPANDEX

220491 **FULL TIGHT**

CONTENT: 7.5 oz. 90% cotton/10% spandex jersey. Charcoal Heather: 7.5 oz. 55% cotton/35% polyester/10% spandex jersey. Gusset lining: Dri-F.I.T.® 100% polyester crepe.

PROFILE: Stretch fit, elasticized waist, lined crotch gusset, turned leg hems, embroidered Swoosh design trademark on left hip.

WHOLESALE: $18.00 **SUGGESTED RETAIL:** $36.00   S   M   L

FIG 238

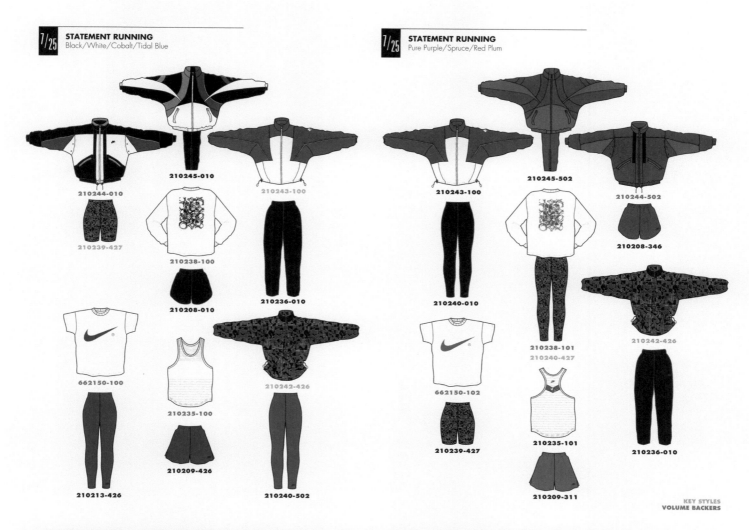

7/25 STATEMENT RUNNING
Black/White/Cobalt/Tidal Blue

7/25 STATEMENT RUNNING
Pure Purple/Spruce/Red Plum

210245-010

210244-010

210243-100

210239-427

210238-100

210236-010

210208-010

662150-100

210235-100

210242-426

210213-426

210209-426

210240-502

210245-502

210243-100

210244-502

210208-346

210240-010

210238-101
210240-427

210242-426

662150-102

210235-101

210236-010

210239-427

210209-311

KEY STYLES
VOLUME BACKERS

FIG 239

236 Cover of Women's Apparel Catalog, Fall 1995

237 Full Tight, Fall 1995

238 Swoosh Full Tight, Fall 1996

239 Page from Women's Apparel Catalog, Fall 1994

FIG 240

FIG 241

211238

240

240

240

FIG 242

DARK PINE	TEAM RED	ROYAL BLUE	VARSITY MAIZE
EVERGREEN	CAVE PURPLE	TIDAL BLUE	DEEP ORANGE
JADE GREEN	HICKORY	FIELD GREEN	COMET RED
LIGHT BRITISH TAN	OBSIDIAN	VARSITY RED	
OLIVE BRONZE	MIDNIGHT NAVY	ULTRAMARINE	
DEEP GREEN	TWILIGHT BLUE	ATLANTIC BLUE	

240 Tech Fundamentals feature, Fall 2000

241 Boot Leg Slacker Tight, Fall 2003

242 Color Palette, Spring 1998

243 Dri-FIT Spandex Vent Tight and Dri-FIT Brushed Black Tight, Holiday 1998

244 Liftsuit, 2001

245 Sphere React feature, Holiday 2005

242

GREYISH

DARK CHARCOAL

LIGHT STONE

UNION GREY

LIGHT BONE

OLIVE GREY

IVORY

LIGHT TAUPE

WHITE

PUTTY

98 *spring Color*

242

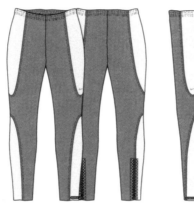

FIG 243

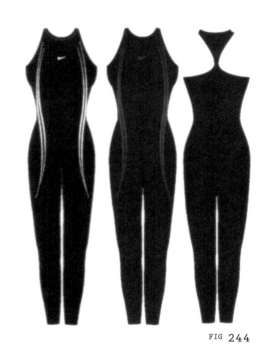

FIG 244

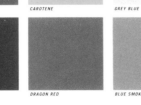

CHLOROPHYL

STEAM

BRIGHT CACTUS

LIGHT SAGE

POOL

CORNSILK

LIGHT CYAN

TOPAZ

ICE

PERSIAN VIOLET

CAROTENE

GREY BLUE

WILD GRAPE

DRAGON RED

BLUE SMOKE

242

FIG 245

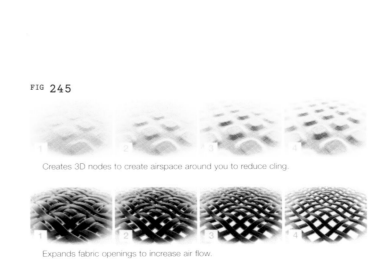

Creates 3D nodes to create airspace around you to reduce cling.

Expands fabric openings to increase air flow.

FIG 246

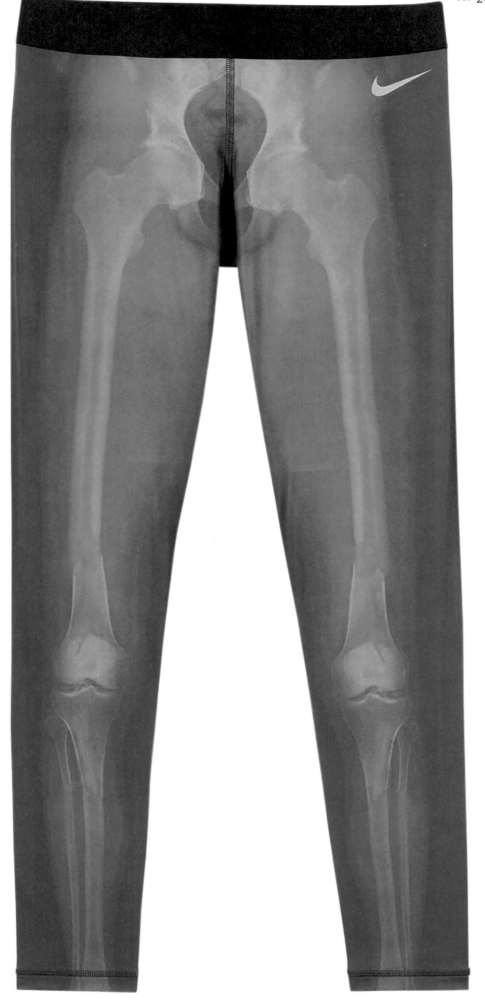

FIG 247

FIG 248

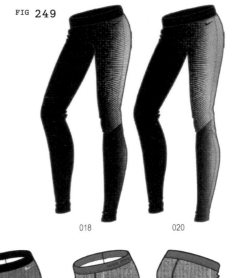

FIG 249

018   020

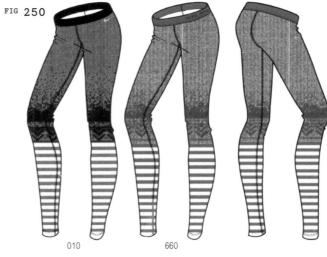

FIG 250

010   660

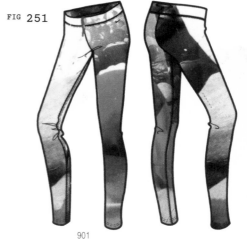

FIG 251

901

FIG 252

010   455

FIG 253

100

249

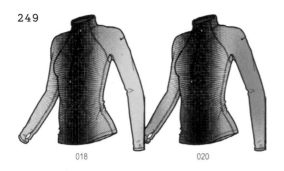

018   020

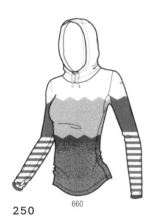

660

250

FIG 254

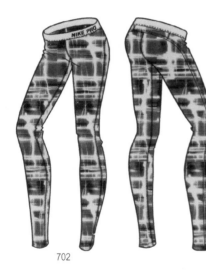

702

043

013

252

FIG 255

248 Pro Energia Vivaz Women's Training Tights, Fall 2014

249 Pro Printed Hyperwarm Tight 2 and Engineered Hyperwarm HZ II, Holiday 2013

250 Hyperwarm Engineered Print Tights and Pro Hyperwarm Engineered Print Hoodie, Holiday 2014

251 Epic Lux Eternity Tights, Spring 2015

252 Epic Run Lux Printed Tights, Spring 2015

253 Legend 2.0 Floe Tight Pant, Spring 2015

254 Pro Printed Tight, Spring 2014

255 HBR Open Hem Pant, Spring 2013

064   201   409

FIG 256

FIG 257

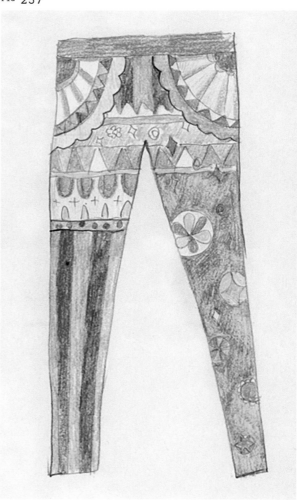

Enter the search term "Tight of the Moment" into the Department of Nike Archives (DNA), and you'll find hundreds of examples of vivid graphic prints in vibrant colors. In 2014 Nike collaborated with Japanese artist Yoko Kanatani to create a playful three-part series that drew on the artist's psyche-delic universe of bright colors and repeated patterns.

256 Tight of the Moment "Sparkling Sunburst," 2014

257 Tight of the Moment "Magical Kaleidoscope" sketches, 2014

257

257

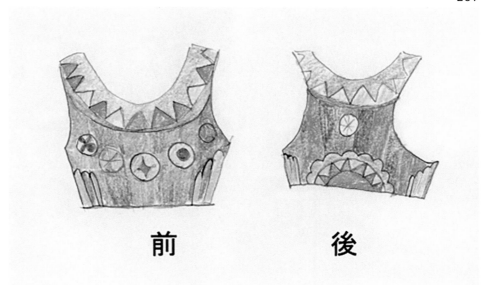

前　　　　　　後

FIG 258

258 Tight of the Moment "Sparkling Sunburst" Sports Bra (detail), 2014

FIG 259

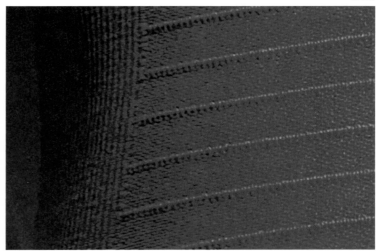

FIG 261

FIG 260

260

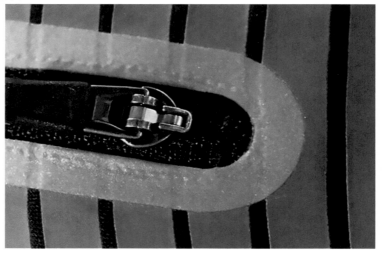

260

FIG 263

FIG 262

261

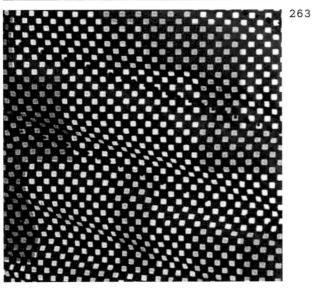

263

259 Zoned Sculpt Tight (detail), Spring 2016

260 Speed Tight (detail), Spring 2016

261 Shieldrunner Jacket, Aeroloft 800 Vest, Shield Tights, Elite Cushion No-Show Tab Socks, Air Max 2016, and Element Sphere Half-Zip Top (detail), Holiday 2015

262 Tight of the Moment, 2016

263 Aeroloft Flash Vest, Dri-Fit Contour Long-Sleeve Shirt, Epic Lux Crop, Elite Cushion No-Show Tab Socks, and Air Zoom Structure 19, Holiday 2015

FIG 264

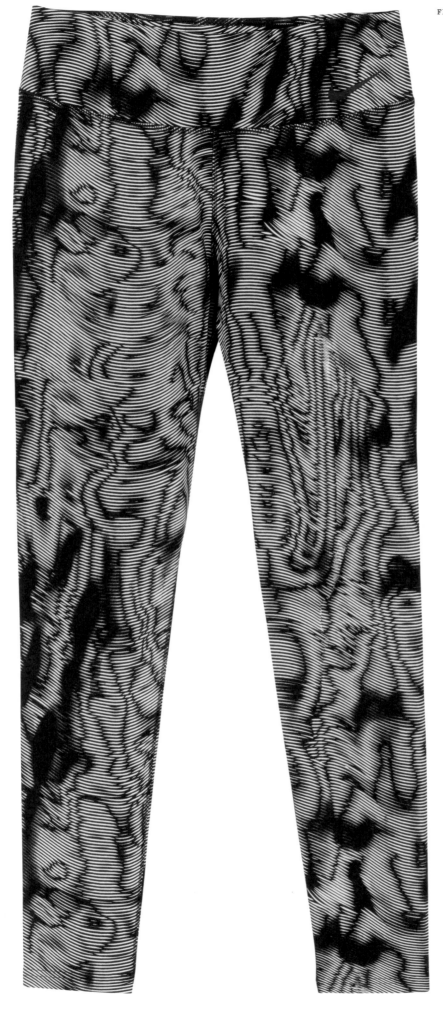

FIG 265

264 Legendary Tight, 2014

265 Bra and Leggings Campaign, 2024

FIG 266

266 Go Leggings with Pockets, 2018

266

266

266

266

266

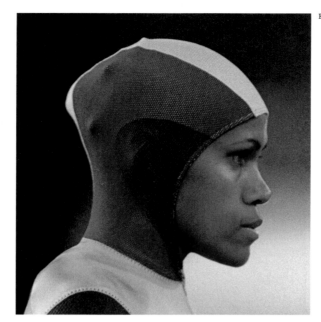

FIG 267

FIG 268

FIG 269

▼

Indigenous Australian athlete Cathy Freeman achieved icon status by winning gold in the 400-meter final at the 2000 Olympic Games in Sydney while wearing the Swift Suit—a one-piece in gray and teal. It featured a hood for maximum effectiveness against drag and fastened under the heels with stirrups, with different fabrics and textures across different body parts to maximize velocity.

FIG **270**

FIG **271**

271

Serena Williams wore a specially made catsuit for both her singles and doubles matches at the 2018 French Open. The black and red one-piece had compressive properties built in to ease the risk of blood clots, which the athlete had suffered since giving birth to her daughter less than one year earlier. Controversy ensued; the French Open banned similar outfits soon afterward. Nike, naturally, responded with an ad campaign. Its tagline read: "You can take the superhero out of her costume, but you can never take away her superpowers."

267 Cathy Freeman wears the Speed Suit at the Olympic Games in Sydney, 2000

268 Cathy Freeman wins the Women's 400m race wearing the Speed Suit at the Olympic Games in Sydney, 2000

269 Australia 2000 Sydney Olympics Swift Suit autographed by Cathy Freeman

270 French Open Catsuit autographed by Serena Williams, 2018

271 Serena Williams at the French Open, 2018

August 21, 2023. Budapest, Hungary.

Dina Asher-Smith makes a strong start in the women's 100-meter semi-final during the World Athletics Championships.

March 30, 2024. San Jose, USA.

Deyna Castellanos takes a free kick for Bay FC against the Houston Dash.

September 29, 2019. Doha, Qatar.

Shelly-Ann Fraser-Pryce runs to victory in the 100-meter sprint at the IAAF World Athletics Championships.

ATHLETE: DINA ASHER-SMITH

SUBJECT: THE LEOTARD

BIOGRAPHY: Dina Asher-Smith is a British sprinter who competes in the 100-, 200-, and 4×100-meter sprints. She was born in 1995 in London, UK.

Performance always comes first.

I used to always race in a crop top and knickers, because my legs need to feel free, but then the leotard came out that fit the same way.

When I raced in it for the first time, I loved it so much.

Until then, I didn't realize how uncomfortable I had felt having my stomach on display.

Particularly in this sport, and in such a male-dominated environment, people feel very free to comment on your body,

and they tend to know nothing about the female anatomy.

We also have to pin on big numbers.

I'm very small; my torso is really compact relative to my legs, so the numbers come from my neck to my belly button.

When I was in a crop top, my numbers didn't even fit on my top;

if I had to pull it down over my stomach, then I couldn't breathe when I was running. It was such a headache.

Now I'm in a leotard,

I can stick the numbers where I want.

I don't have to worry about the paper cutting my neck in the blocks.

ATHLETE: DEYNA CASTELLANOS

SUBJECT: UNIFORM

BIOGRAPHY: Deyna Castellanos is a Venezuelan footballer. She
was born in 1999 in Maracay, Venezuela.

198

I want to feel strong and sexy when I'm training, and if I look good, I feel good.

When I put on a jersey, I feel powerful.

It's our time to rock.

That's what we prepare for all week, and it's the most important part of the week.

Wearing the uniform feels very special.

It's finally game time.

That's why we're here.

That's why we sacrifice so much during the week—it's just to enjoy this ninety minutes of football.

And so that other people can enjoy it too.

ATHLETE: SHELLY-ANN FRASER-PRYCE

SUBJECT: HAIR

I hear a lot of, 'Isn't your hair too much when you're running?'

I say, 'No, because that's not what I'm thinking about.'

When I look in the mirror and my hair is laid, it's bright and colorful, I'm feeling at my best, and I perform at my best.

My hair for me is a superpower.

It's me changing into my work outfit.

When you see me off the track and my hair is black, it's Shelly-Ann.

When I'm on the track and my hair is colored, with bows and ribbons, my nails are colored,

that's my alter ego.

We Jamaicans are very vibrant; we are a prideful country.

Every year when we have Jamaica Day here, the girls are wearing yellow and green braids and dressing up as Shelly-Ann.

To me that's powerful.

A small island like Jamaica is a dot on the map, but when we step on the track, it's a whole other level.

You don't have to question where I'm from when you see me.

ATHLETE: XOCHILT HOOVER

SUBJECT: MODESTY

BIOGRAPHY: Xochilt Hoover is a Nike yoga instructor of Nicaraguan descent. She was born
in 1986 in Texas, USA.

My mother's Latina, and modesty played a big part in how I was raised.

Clothing doesn't have to be revealing in order to feel beautiful.

Learning to own that has been part of my journey.

At some point, I decided I was representing out there for bodies that are

softer and curvier and still really strong.

It's not that I'm ashamed of any of these parts of my body, but I feel more comfortable when they are more covered.

Being a yoga teacher, I thought I was already very connected to my body,

but now I have that added element of how I'm being perceived.

Flowy and comfortable is my practice fit for yoga.

There's a lot of checking in with your body and your breath,

and letting your belly be soft.

That's why I think letting the clothes channel that ease and flow is important.

the body:

seen

heather radke

I'm not a regular runner. I haven't run a race since high school, and I don't count weekly miles. I have no aspirations to run a marathon or even a 5K. But sometimes, when the weather gets nice, or I'm feeling anxious, or I just get the urge, I decide to jog a few times around the park near my Brooklyn apartment. In that way, running is easy. You don't need much of anything to do it—no gym membership, special equipment, or other people. It is a democratic form of exercise, one that is available to most of us and can be done almost anywhere. All you have to do is walk out your front door and put one foot in front of the other.

The one thing you do need is clothing. I keep half a drawer in my dresser for the kind of clothes I might run in—if it's cold, I wear yoga pants; if it's hot, I wear bike shorts. I throw on a sports bra and a T-shirt. I lace up a pair of sneakers. These clothes are designed to allow for movement and flexibility. The pants stretch, and the sports bra holds me tight. The effect of the outfit is that I feel both supported and free. I'm able to move fluidly, painlessly. The promise of running clothes is that the person wearing them will be able to focus on their stride and their footfall, their body moving through space. We won't have to think much at all about how we look.

But, of course, a woman moving through the world is never fully granted that freedom. It's almost impossible not to be aware of how I look or how I compare to others. The inner monologue is always there: Have I hidden the parts of my body I'm most ashamed of? Are my thighs jiggling? Are my breasts bouncing? Have I revealed too much? Is that man looking at me? Are these shorts too tight? Should I suck in my stomach (but then how will I breathe)? Do I look foolish? I worry that I will be revealed to be as out of shape as I actually am and that I will seem silly for running at all. I worry about being leered at, and I worry that I'm getting too old and flabby to ever be leered at again.

These are feelings born of insecurity and honed over a lifetime of feeling observed and judged. And they are feelings that most women—including me—work to manage through fashion and dress. Curious about how other women feel about their clothes when they run, I put out a call on Instagram: "Are you a woman who runs (even just every once in a while)? Let me know if you'd be up for answering questions about what you wear!" When anyone expressed interest, I sent along a short list of questions.

Answers came in from as far away as Australia and climates as disparate as snowy northern Michigan and sunny Los Angeles. Some women ran several marathons a year; others had never run a race in their lives. Some had been running for more than twenty years; others only started running seriously a few years before, trying to manage post-baby bulge or middle-age ennui. I heard from women in their twenties, thirties, forties, and fifties; white women, Asian women, and Black women; women who worked lucrative professional jobs and women who were unemployed. It was by no means a scientific sample, but it was a diverse one. Nearly everyone who responded seemed surprised to find out that they held so many feelings about their own running gear, and that so much complex thinking about factors such as weather, fashion, and femininity went into answering the seemingly basic question: what should I wear to run?

COMFORT

"The number one thing I'm concerned about when running is comfort," Jill, a woman in her early forties who runs in races several times a year, told me. And although this sentiment was almost universally expressed, just what was meant by *comfort* differed for everyone. The word chafe came up in nearly everyone's answer—the inescapable enemy of the runner—as did the myriad ways runners contend with weather conditions. *Comfort* sometimes meant fleece-lined leggings for winter runs, and other times, it meant short shorts and no shirts for humid Florida days when the sweat refuses to evaporate.

At its most basic, *comfort* means that the garments on your body won't hurt you and that they will act as a barrier between you and the environment. Comfortable clothes are supposed to allow you to move your body. The idea that athletic clothes would need to meet these requirements seems utterly obvious, but it was, in fact, hard-won, particularly for women athletes. It was only at the end of the nineteenth century that women in the West began wearing clothing that was designed for physical activity.

The first athletic clothes designed specifically for women were bloomers —puffy, pantaloon-type garments that separated the legs but still bore a resemblance to a skirt. It was in these pants that women first exercised in public—going to gym class, sitting astride bicycles, even playing on baseball teams. It's hard to overstate how upsetting these funny cotton pants were to Victorian sensibilities. In 1895 the *New York Sun* suggested the bloomer-wearing woman was "riding to the devil" and that the fad was "born of infidelity." Many mayors banned women from playing baseball in their towns (a popular fad in the 1880s and 1890s) because their attire was considered indecent. Others just thought bloomers were ugly, calling them "homely" and "mannish."

A tricky contradiction, bloomers were perceived as unfeminine and gender-bending yet somehow also suggestive and excessively sexual. They both obscured femininity—taking a woman out of her "correct" place as a domestic, hobbled skirt-wearer—and enhanced it in the most troublesome ways. To put it bluntly, pants make it unambiguous that a woman has two legs, and those legs converge someplace, and that that place is a woman's crotch. It was the very fact of women's sexuality—that she might have sex, might be sexual, and might be running around a baseball diamond at the same time—that upset so many at the turn of the twentieth century.

This Victorian-era angst would weave its way through the story of women's sports for the next one hundred years or more. It's also baked into the question so many of us ask when we decide what clothes to wear on a jog. We want to be comfortable in the sense that we want to be able to move our legs freely and maintain a regular and healthy body temperature, but we also want to feel comfortable in other ways. We want to be safe. We want to be at ease. And many of us want to be covered up and, to the best of our abilities, desexualized.

EXPOSURE

"The very idea of wearing shorts when I exercise makes me shiver," Madeleine, a relatively new runner in her thirties from Australia, told me. "It's somehow the most exposing or vulnerable thing I could think of wearing. Something to do with all that skin being touchable?" Madeleine was describing a problem that women runners have faced since the earliest days of women's competitive running, one that is perpetually difficult to solve.

For much of the history of women's professional sports, female athletes pushed for the right to expose more of their bodies. This was not because they were eager to appear sexy while competing but because they were simply trying to move. They did not want to contend with giant skirts or poofy bloomers as they ran. Instead, they wanted what the men had: clothes that would allow them the freedom to compete at the height of their ability.

By 1928 women track athletes had finally won a version of what they were after—they began to compete in men's running shorts, which were loose, billowy, short, and made from a flexible synthetic material. Women

They wanted what the men had:

clothes that would allow them the freedom to compete at the height of their ability.

"I think there's an interesting division between 'showing skin' and 'showing shape.'"

track athletes wore something resembling those same shorts for almost sixty years. For most of this time, the shorts they wore had been designed for men; athletic shorts created specifically for women didn't exist until the late 1970s.

Although these shorts at first elicited considerable anxiety—like bloomers, the early years of women in track shorts drummed up fears of both hypersexuality and dangerously masculinized women—they eventually became accepted and then mundane. By the 1970s, the popularization of bikinis and miniskirts made track shorts seem tame, and Title IX helped to normalize the notion of female athletes. What had once seemed an almost freakish aberration had become run-of-the-mill.

The multi-decade reign of men's track shorts on female athletes only ended in the 1980s, with the sudden proliferation of "buns"—very short shorts that were, essentially, bikini bottoms. By the 1988 Olympics, most women track-and-field athletes were wearing buns. By the 1992 Olympics, they all were. Often when a component of an athletic uniform changes so widely and so quickly, it is assumed that it helps with performance. But buns didn't seem to provide any such advantage. If they had, men would have worn them too. For some athletes, the advantage was psychological—they described feeling fast, sleek, and unencumbered by fabric. For others, buns signaled the frank sexualization of the sport—a sartorial rejoinder for the endless suggestions that a woman who runs or vaults or jumps isn't sufficiently feminine.

For almost a century, women runners had pushed cultural norms so that they could expose their bodies. But in the twenty-first century, many have been demanding what Madeleine craves when she runs: coverage. In 2021 the Norwegian women's beach handball team refused to wear the required bikini bottoms in competition because they felt sexualized and physically uncomfortable. In the same year, the German women's gymnastics team opted to wear full-body unitards instead of leotards as they competed in the Olympic trials to push against the sexualization of that sport. Competitive track athletes, too, have begun to adopt clothing that prioritizes comfort and coverage; only one of the four members of the US women's 4x100 meters relay team at the 2016 Olympics wore buns.

For many of the runners who wrote to me, this threat of exposure—skin being available to be seen, touched, and leered at—was a powerful motivator for deciding what to wear on a run. Many described making choices to wear baggy clothes, or longer pants and shirts, to fight the vulnerability that comes when skin is on display. One way that many women manage this feeling of excessive exposure is to wear running tights. Unlike shorts, tights can be a way to be both covered and exposed. "I think there's an interesting division between 'showing skin' and 'showing shape,'" explained Sarah, a runner from L.A. "And because tights can do more shaping work, they can be both more revealing and more concealing." When you wear tights, or even tight shorts, anyone can see your curves. But the material holds you in and hides your flesh, which can offer a comforting feeling of containment and control.

The tension between the need to move and the fear of overexposure is fundamental for women athletes. In fact, it is a question that often feels like it is at the heart of the female experience: When do I want to reveal my body, and when do I prefer, or need, to conceal it? And while sometimes the answer comes in response to worry about how we appear—whether our bodies will be judged, whether our thighs are jiggling—many of us are also trying to grapple with something more fundamental: our physical safety.

For most of us, running happens in public, either outside or in the gym. Our bodies enter the complexity of the communal space and the many people who occupy it, and our clothes are a crucial part of how we contend with what we find there.

Andrea, a woman in her forties who lives in New Jersey, simultaneously fears drawing too much attention and not enough. "To be honest, there are sometimes public safety reports that pop up in our town, so I often think about wanting to draw less attention," she said. Because of this, she wears clothes that cover all of her skin. She also worries about the danger of sharing the road with vehicles and not drawing *enough* attention. "I sometimes go running pretty early in the morning before sunrise, so I got very into finding and wearing reflective or bright-colored clothes," she said.

Michelle, who runs in northern Michigan, described preparing for a very specific part of her run where she is exposed to cars and people. "I have a trail near my house that is pretty quiet, but there is a stretch of my run on a very busy street. I feel really aware of my clothing choices while on that half mile. Not a lot of people run in my community, so I think I am noticeable." She went on to say, "There have been times when I've been harassed by men shouting out their windows as they drive by or as I run by their house. Or when I'm doing a track workout and the whole middle school boys' football team shows up."

For these women, their clothes must protect them—not only from the elements but from the unpredictability of other people. It's something women have asked of their running clothes for a long time.

One of the most famous examples of a woman who found protection in her running outfit happened by accident. When Kathrine Switzer became the first woman to compete in the Boston Marathon officially in 1967, she wore a gray sweatsuit over a burgundy running top and carefully ironed track shorts. It was a cold, sleety day, and she made the sartorial choice because of the weather. But her choice had the additional effect of obscuring the fact that she was a woman from a distance, which let her begin the race without officials realizing they'd inadvertently given a woman official racing numbers. When it dawned on a male official that Switzer wasn't a man, he pulled at her sweatsuit, trying to disrobe her and reveal her gender. Although Switzer asserts that she wasn't trying to hide anything, the clothes functioned as a suit of armor. They kept her safe and allowed her to finish the race.

Switzer's story reinforces those of Michelle and Andrea (and surely many others), who have to weigh not only factors of weather and fashion when they suit up for a run but what it means for a woman's body to enter public space, particularly when she is on her own. The ability to cover up or expose can offer a sense of control in a moment when there is little feeling of agency. But it's also true that when cars and men and horns lurk, clothes can only do so much.

Running was a mode of freedom, an opportunity to feel unbounded.

Runners make decisions about what to wear based on practicality, comfort, safety, and exposure. But there's at least one more reason why women wear what they do to run: style.

There is perhaps no other athlete who embodies this opportunity for expression more than one of the fastest women ever recorded: sprinter Florence Griffith Joyner. Flo-Jo's style defied all previous notions of what was possible and acceptable for an athlete to wear. Her one-woman transformation of athletic fashion began in the early 1980s, when she adopted one-legged fuchsia or metallic leggings—buns on one side, unitard on the other. She later donned all-lace leggings and a glowing white bodysuit that made her look like a runaway bride sprinting from the chapel and her jilted fiancé. At the 1988 Olympics, she wore a red leotard with a black-and-red hood that conjured a powerful, beautiful robot. While her incredible athletic ability spoke for itself, she added flamboyant personal style to assert her femininity, strength, and even joy.

As a Black athlete, these style choices were beautifully transgressive. Black women athletes had long endured an extreme version of the stereotypes wielded at all women runners, assuming them to be either hypersexual or insufficiently feminine. Flo-Jo vibrantly pushed against those stereotypes by refusing to fit into one fashion narrative, oscillating from high femme to cyberpunk to aerobics chic as she saw fit. Her look influenced a generation of athletes from Sha'Carri Richardson to Serena Williams and proved that track clothes could be more than just a practical choice.

But it's not just professional athletes who crave what style and fashion can offer. Many of the women I spoke with described the boost that colorful, vibrant running clothes can offer. "I feel most powerful in clothes that draw people's attention, like bold colors, something that fits just right, something unique," explained Kristi, a runner from Portland, Oregon. Jill, who often wears neutrals when she trains, craves attention and vibrancy on race day: "I want to feel like a superhero, and I want the encouragement of crowds yelling for me, so I wear the brightest colors possible, and I tape my name on my shirt." These runners follow in the strides of Flo-Jo; their radiant shorts help them feel formidable, capable, and strong.

On a recent gray day in late January, I went for a run. After a week of days below freezing, it was finally in the forties. My toddler was taking a nap, my husband was doing the dishes, and I realized that I had a couple of hours before needing to do anything in particular. I could have rested, worked, or read, but instead, I decided to run. I pulled on my thickest yoga pants—the ones I wore throughout my pregnancy, the ones that have pockets for my phone and keys, the ones that hug my body but not too tightly. I grabbed a T-shirt, sweatshirt, and a thin pair of gloves and stepped outside into the cold. It had been a few months since I'd been on a run, and I knew I'd quickly feel winded and out of shape. But my hope was that I'd also feel something else.

I wanted to feel like I did when I was a little girl running across our backyard or down the street, playing tag, or trying to get to a friend's house as fast as I could. In those days, running was a way to get from here to there, a way to feel fast and strong. I didn't think much about what I was wearing or how I was supposed to look. In those years before self-consciousness fully took hold, running was a mode of freedom, an opportunity to feel unbounded.

Madeline from Australia described it this way: "I want to feel like a gazelle or other fast creature (I am not a fast runner, but that doesn't matter) that can't be grasped or caught." Diana, a runner from Brooklyn, described the freedom she feels another way: "When running is working for me, it's a chance to be in my body rather than thinking about how it looks or having feelings about it."

Lulu, a forty-one-year-old journalist from Chicago who runs in spandex leggings, said that she loves to run because, for once, she's not thinking about other people or what they think of her. "Hypnotized by endorphins and fresh air and horizon, I'm outside whizzing past people," she said. "I feel like they can't catch me, even with their gaze." She explained that wearing spandex shorts lets her feel only her body and her muscles—there is no fabric swishing around to remind her of the external world. She can be covered and nude at the same time; she can forget she is a self with boundaries and limits. Running, for this woman who has been doing it for twenty-five years, is a "rare fucking break" from limits. And she wants to wear clothes that let her feel limitless.

Limitlessness, I think, is what underlies the desire to run for so many women, and it is what we want most from the clothes we wear. The history of track shorts, and really the history of women running, is about a quest to feel fast, free, and uncatchable. When running clothes work best, they allow a woman to feel safe but also uncontained. They help her to feel free from the fears that are fundamental to what it is to be a woman—fears of being looked at, judged, and even hurt. And although there is nothing that clothes can do to actually transcend the fundamental oppression of women that underlies those fears, they can help us feel safer, more colorful, less chafed, cooler, and even more (or less) visible. They can allow us to step out the door and feel our bodies first, even for just a minute, instead of the gaze of others.

4

the body:

owned

Celebrating female athletes means celebrating the

female body.

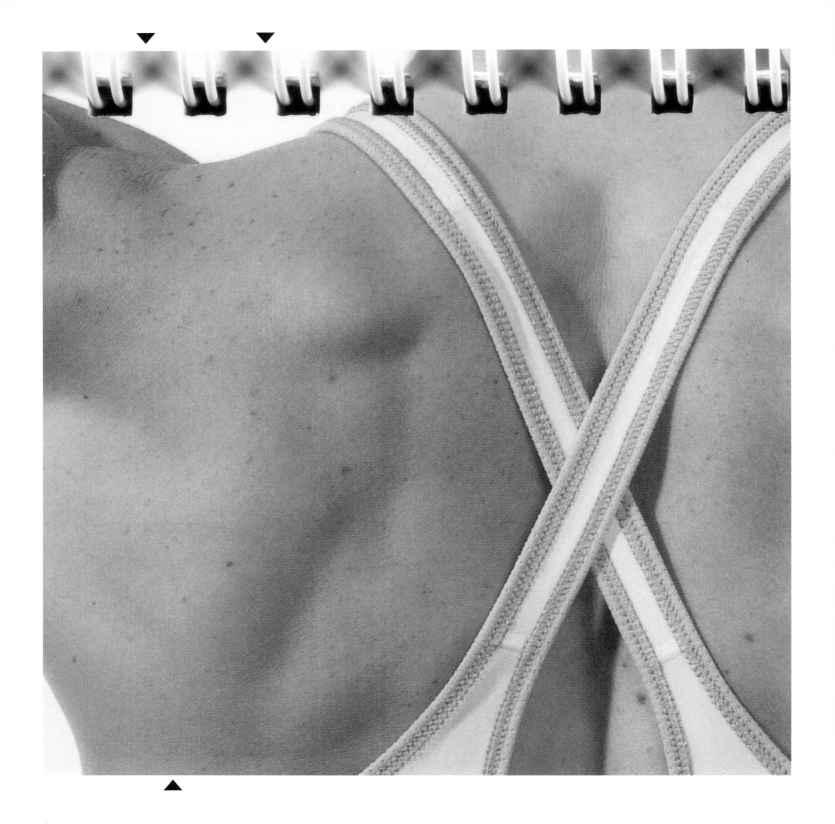

sports

bra

FIG 272

It's July 10, 1999, and 90,185 spectators have packed into California's Rose Bowl stadium to watch the FIFA Women's World Cup final. (It's a new international record for attendance at a women's sporting event—and forty million more Americans are watching on TV.) The United States and China reach full-time with a 0–0 draw, which continues into a tense penalty shoot-out. With China scoring only four of their five penalty kicks, defender Brandi Chastain steps up to take the decisive fifth attempt for the US and duly scores, clinching the title for the hosts. A split second after the goal lands, she swoops her jersey up and over her head in a gesture of total exaltation, celebration, and liberation, exposing a black sports bra with a tiny Nike swoosh on the front.

"When the laundry gets low, I wear it," Chastain told Jeré Longman of the *New York Times* of that bra in an interview at her home four years later. "It still works, you know. It's not a one-time deal."[1] The bra in question was a prototype from the Inner Actives line, which would launch two months later. The Department of Nike Archives (DNA) holds a similar piece, signed by Chastain (the original being still, presumably, in the athlete's possession). It is made from a blend of Dri-FIT microfiber and spandex, with a mesh-front lining and elasticized bottom hem. It retailed for thirty-two dollars. It's not unlikely that you have a similar version in your own closet. Still, its exposure in this watershed moment for women's football sparked an outpouring of emotion: jubilation, fury, disgust.

The United States' World Cup win came pre-Y2K (2000), pre-Facebook (2004), and pre-iPhone (2007). In sports, it had been twenty-seven years since Title IX passed in the United States in 1972. The landmark federal civil rights law prohibited sex-based discrimination at any government-funded institution, and in so doing, it granted women greater access to sports-based collegiate scholarships and increased opportunities on competitive stages.

Chastain was one of the 99ers—the first generation to grow up with the right to play—and her winning goal was a serendipitous moment in a year of subtle but important shifts for the sports bra. In fact, 1999 marked the culmination of an evolution in sports bra design that had been happening quietly in Beaverton, Oregon, for many years.

First, however, came semantics. Although Nike had already spent more than two decades working to equip female athletes, by 1999, the language required to talk about their physiological needs presented

272 New Crossback Bra, Holiday 2000

273 *Sports Illustrated* Cover, Winter 1999

274 Cover of Women's Apparel Catalog (detail), Spring 2001

275 Color Palette, Summer 2000

FIG 273

FIG 274

FIG 275

NOMADIC GREEN

275

MYSTIC TEAL

FIG 276

FIG 277

FIG 278

OBSIDIAN

VAPOR

The bra Brandi Chastain was wearing when she scored the winning goal in the 1999 FIFA Women's World Cup final was a prototype from Nike's Inner Actives line, which would launch two months later. Some believed her shirt-off celebration to be a marketing ploy by the brand—it wasn't, though Chastain did have a contract with Nike. In fact, the defensive player hadn't been expected to score at all, let alone the winning goal; she had changed out of her first, sweat-soaked bra and into this one, with its comparatively small swoosh, at halftime.

276 Brandi Chastain celebreates scoring the winning penalty in the final of the FIFA Women's World Cup, 1999

277 Cover of Women's Apparel Catalog (detail), Fall 1999

278 Color Palette, Summer 2000

279 Inner Actives Racer Back Sport Bra autographed by Brandi Chastain, 1999

a greater issue than the company's design and innovation teams could solve. Throughout the 1970s and 1980s, referring aloud to the bra, much less the breast, was simply too large a sociological hurdle for the United States' primarily male sales force to overcome. The breast was to be concealed and ignored or sexualized and objectified. There was no middle ground. Nike didn't use the word *bra* publicly in a product name until 1996.

Photographs of Chastain's celebration quickly proliferated, covering magazines, newspapers, and news outlets. The response was enormous. Some felt her bare-bellied celebration marked a kind of emancipation. Why shouldn't a woman celebrate like a man? It wasn't until 2004 that FIFA banned the removal of shirts on the field; now violators are reprimanded with a yellow card. Others thought it a blatant insinuation of a collaboration with the brand. (It wasn't, although Chastain did have a contract with Nike. In fact, the defensive player hadn't been expected to score at all, let alone the winning goal; she had changed out of her first, sweat-soaked bra and into this one, with its comparatively small logo, at halftime.)

Whatever the cause of the outrage—the progress of one woman, or of all women everywhere—naysayers were all but drowned out by the more than forty million fans who cheered while witnessing it, and the many millions more who saw coverage soon afterward, and in it an athlete they could aspire to emulate. Around the world, audiences recognized that celebrating female athletes meant celebrating the female body.

For many women, sports are not possible without a sports bra. Breast tissue sits on muscle but is not supported by muscle. As a woman runs, her breasts move in a figure-eight motion, with the overall movement having a drastic impact on surrounding soft tissue. Without any, or adequate, support, women move more cautiously, turning the body less, shortening the gait. The movement of the breasts causes pain. This pain slows female athletes down and limits their athletic expression, with untold ramifications for the body.

But women have always moved. There has been a demand for underwear that permitted a more athletic life since at least the 1890s, when "health corsets"—more flexible and comfortable than their rigid forebears—became popular for use during bicycling, itself a revolution. "With the growing use of bicycles, a nationwide craze that started in the 1880s, these less restrictive corsets were meant to give women greater freedom and mobility whenever they took to 'the wheel,'" wrote Cathy Keen, archivist at the Smithsonian National Museum of American History.[2] She continued, "Bicycles not only offered a means of transportation

277

FIG 279

and leisure; they also gave women independence. The new type of corset . . . also promised freedom of movement for women as they engaged in the physical activities of daily life."

In 1977, a little less than a century after the introduction of the health corset, costume designers Hinda Miller, Lisa Lindahl, and Polly Palmer Smith came together in search of a solution to the insufficient support an everyday brassiere provided for running. American track-and-field coach Bill Bowerman had published *Jogging: A Physical Fitness Program for All Ages* in 1967 (three years after he and Phil Knight had founded Blue Ribbon Sports, soon to be Nike, Inc.). By the mid-1970s, jogging had swept the nation, and Lindahl's sister, Victoria Woodrow, was an enthusiastic and undersupported subscriber. Together, the three designers created a number of early prototypes of the sports bra. They found them lacking each time until—upon the suggestion of Lindahl's husband—they stitched together two men's athletic supporters to create a garment that had stretch, support, and movement incorporated within it. The first example of the resulting prototype—initially named the Jock Bra but quickly renamed the Jogbra—is still held in the Smithsonian's collection today. The irony is almost too much—women's support is secondary to men's, even when it comes to their underwear. But the difficulties the Jogbra encountered in the world at large were the same as those faced by all sports brands: stores didn't know how to market it; salesmen (and they were principally men) didn't know how to sell it.

During the 1980s, as both second-wave feminism and the studio fitness craze took hold of contemporary culture, attitudes toward women's sports and the clothing they wore to do them shifted. Clothing became tighter, shinier and bodies more exposed, and with this shift, female sexuality became more apparent, irrepressible. Unitards, bodysuits, and crop tops became part and parcel of fitness culture: clothing designed both to encourage its owners to create sculpted bodies and, having done so, to showcase them.

At Nike, against this backdrop, the first product to tout a built-in support bra was the Airborne, a top that debuted quietly in the fall 1986 catalog. Made from a blend of polyester, cotton, and Lycra, with a Lycra and nylon lining, it was designed to fit like a crop top—underwear moonlighting as outerwear—and was released in six colorways: white, tropic blue, canary, red, gray heather, and black.

But if the presentation of a garment that at last provided breast support was understated, its reception by athletes and amateurs alike was not. It was such a hit that during the making of the 1988 ad "It's a Woman's

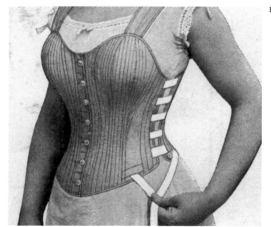

FIG 280

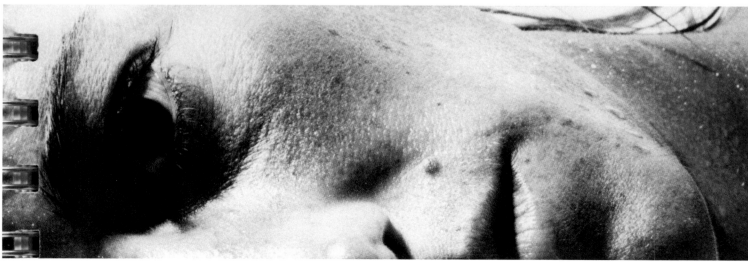

FIG 281

222

FIG 282

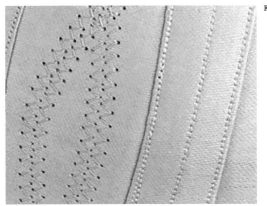

280 Ferris' Good Sense Corset Waist For Bicycle Wear ad, 1889

281 Cover of Women's Apparel Catalog (detail), Fall 1999

282 Dr Warner's Corset, c. 1889

DESCRIPTION OF INVENTION

WHAT TO INCLUDE IN YOUR DESCRIPTION:
What it is. What it is for. How it works. How it achieves its purpose. Name of invention. Materials used (if known).

THE PRODUCT IS THE FIRST ATHLETIC SUPPORTER FOR WOMEN: IT IS CALLED THE "JOCK BRA."

IT IS A BRASSIERE THAT HOLDS THE BREASTS FIRMLY AGAINST THE BODY TO MINIMIZE ANY MOVEMENT THAT MAY CAUSE DISCOMFORT. AT THE SAME TIME IT IS DESIGNED FOR COMFORT, HAS PERSPIRATION-ABSORBING PROPERTIES, AND STRAPS THAT WILL NOT SLIP OFF THE SHOULDER NO MATTER HOW VIGOROUS THE ACTIVITY IS THAT THE ATHELETE IS ENGAGED IN.

THERE IS NO "HARDWARE" (clasps, hooks, etc.) ON THIS BRA. IT ACHIEVES ITS PURPOSE THROUGH ITS UNIQUE DESIGN. AS A WOMAN WHO RUNS (4 mi/day) I PERSONALLY FELT THE NEED FOR A BRA THAT "SECURED" MY BREAST MOVEMENT. THERE WERE NONE TO BE FOUND ON THE PRESENT MARKET THAT I FELT WERE SATISFACTORY. AFTER TALKING TO OTHER WOMEN RUNNERS I DISCERNED THAT I WAS NOT ALONE IN THIS SEARCH FOR AN ADEQUATE ATHLETIC BRASSIERE.

HENCE, THE UNIQUE DESIGN GREW DIRECTLY OUT OF WHAT I FELT I NEEDED & WANTED FOR SUPPORT IN A BRA.

ITS MAIN UNIQUENESS IS ITS ABILITY TO "BIND" — TO HOLD THE BREASTS FIRMLY AGAINST THE BODY — WHILE REMAINING COMFORTABLE & LIGHTWEIGHT.

MATERIALS USED:

CHARBERT FABRICS
STYLE #3871/170 COTTON & LYCRA
6.97 per yard 70" WIDE
INTERNATIONAL STRETCH
#2822 2" 15½¢ per yd
#5074 ½" 5¼¢ per yd

FIG 283

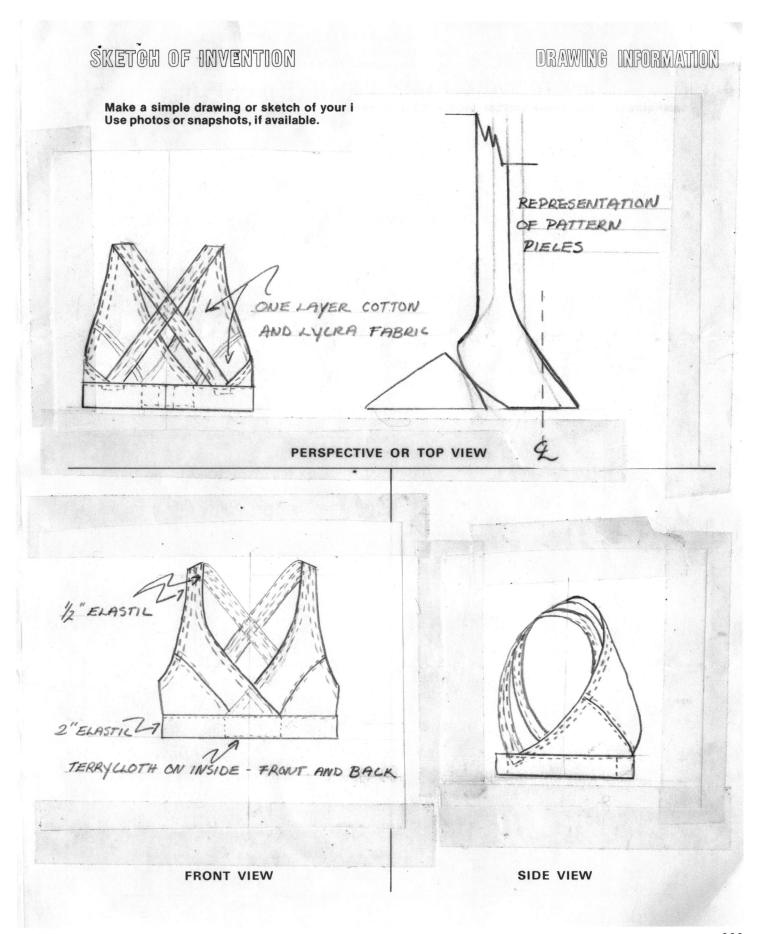

**Make a simple drawing or sketch of your i
Use photos or snapshots, if available.**

ONE LAYER COTTON AND LYCRA FABRIC

REPRESENTATION OF PATTERN PIECES

PERSPECTIVE OR TOP VIEW

½" ELASTIC

2" ELASTIC

TERRYCLOTH ON INSIDE - FRONT AND BACK

FRONT VIEW

SIDE VIEW

283

The Jogbra was designed by Hinda Miller, Lisa Lindahl, and Polly Palmer Smith in 1977, one year before Nike launched its apparel division. Together, the three designers created a number of early prototypes of the sports bra and found them lacking each time until—upon the suggestion of Lindahl's husband—they stitched together two men's athletic supporters. The first example of the resulting prototype—initially named the Jock Bra but quickly renamed the Jogbra—is still held in the Smithsonian's collection today.

283 Jogbra record and disclosure of invention, 1997

FIG 284

FIG 285

FIG 286

NY-SGMA-1981

Prerogative," cross-training athlete Joanne Ernst told DNA that she was beyond thrilled to get her hands on something approaching a sports bra. Previously she had been forced to wear swimsuits to minimize breast pain while moving; in the designs presented to her to wear on the shoot, she saw an alternative. (Others were similarly enthused that day, as the stylists struggled to keep hold of the Airborne. Many athletes left with them at the end of the production.)

Names are powerful, however, and it took time for Nike to call a bra a bra. For almost a decade, a series of variations on the Airborne followed, but always with names such as the Running Airborne, Fitness Top, or Racerback. Until 1994, when the silence that had cloaked the word was finally broken with the appearance of the Bra Top in Nike's spring catalog. The subtle but watershed moment marked a new era, one of transparency, dialogue, research, and innovation. Five years later, Brandi Chastain's World Cup–winning goal, and the ensuing celebration, shook off the shame surrounding it altogether.

A new attitude to the bra meant a new attitude to the breasts that filled it. In September 1999, a few months after Chastain's goal, Nike launched its Inner Actives bra range with a set of print ads that put nude breasts on full display. Double-page spreads ran in national and global publications. "After years of exercise, what kind of shape will your breasts be in?" asked bold sans serif type. The collection marked Nike's first application of innovative and extensive research into the sports bra. Perhaps more importantly, it opened the door for a dialogue between brand and consumer about what women really required, and how best to provide it.

That dialogue continues today. Since the inception of women's apparel at the company, Nike has been associated with solving problems for elite athletes, making the kinds of incremental shifts that, in professional sports, have had an extraordinary impact. The challenges now are what they have always been: Manage sweat. Eradicate chafing. Maintain comfort. Provide support in whatever form it is needed, or wanted, and total freedom of movement. Allow wearers to express themselves, showing up in the world exactly the way they want to. But the intention has changed. In recent years, Nike has established a commitment to take the innovation and insight gleaned through a history of working in sport, and use it to solve the everyday problems of athletes. *Athlete* meaning anybody with a body.

What does that look like in practice? If, at its origin, the sports bra was created to serve a slim, small-breasted, middle-distance runner, its manifestation today is considerably more inclusive—and continuing to diversify, which it perhaps will do in perpetuity. From an execution standpoint, short of every individual having a bespoke garment, there is no such thing as a perfect bra. Instead, Nike is committed to designing bras which can be worn for every stage of a person's life and every experience: adolescence, pregnancy, breastfeeding, perimenopause, regardless of gender.

For the design team, it begins and ends with the athlete. In the past five years, the company has redefined how it addresses fit, comfort, and support for different body sizes and shapes across the board. Body-mapping, computational design, bra-bots, and other advances in technology all have their part to play in the design process—but at its core, this shift means spending more time with all different kinds of people, with all different kinds of needs. The team wear-tests every development rigorously to ensure the proper fit for bodies of different sizes and shapes, different levels of support, different social and cultural concerns. Consumer feedback is actioned immediately, confirming or altering what designers found to be true and helping them to customize solutions for each piece across the entire range. Simply put, the more people a collection is tested on, the more people it will serve.

This attention starts at the beginning of the need for a sports bra. Research shows that young women who stop taking part in sports usually do so around the ages of ten to twelve. During this coming-of-age period, a monumental shift in physicality and emotion takes place, demanding an adjustment to a whole new way of moving through the world. Breast development and connected issues can present an insurmountable challenge for young people who might otherwise have gone on to break records and make history. Nike is uniquely positioned to address the dropout that occurs at this stage, using innovation and education to make breast development less of a barrier to an active life.

As for maternity: The Nike (M) collection launched in 2020. As is true of all the products in the collection, the sports bras were developed out of existing, well-loved Nike products, signifying that becoming

284 Jogbra prototype

285 Jogbra production model

286 Jogbra Inc stall, New York, 1981

FIG 287

a mother doesn't mean the end of life as an athlete. Pregnancy and postpartum are periods of remarkable physiological change; the bra is specially designed to accommodate fluctuating body sizes. An adjustable band expands as the growing fetus encourages the internal organs up and into the rib cage. Clips above each cup allow for discreet nursing or pumping—acknowledging that the needs of athletes who are also mothers resonate beyond the track, the field, or the court. The fabric is "no-show" (meaning leaked milk is not visible from the outside), moisture-wicking, and soft against sensitive skin. The collection was designed to support athlete mothers throughout their pregnancy and postpartum period, whatever that might look like and however long it might last.

Only two decades divided the World Cups of 1999 and 2019, when the present age of bra design began in earnest. But if you looked up from the middle of a game during the latter, you might have found yourself face-to-face with a billboard or a magazine spread headlined with the words: "No sports bra, no sport." The message echoed across all of Nike's marketing channels throughout the tournament. No ambivalence around the use of the word *bra* to be found here—nor about the women it was created to support.

The slogan remains powerful because it remains true. It has underpinned several decades of the most rigorous research and development in bras the sports industry has seen, and it is especially true at Nike, an organization fixed on pushing the boundaries of what is believed possible and making the results accessible to everybody.

With every year, new research is carried out. With every year, bra design improves. With every year, more women find the support they need to move in Nike. That in itself is a victory worth celebrating—shirt on or shirt off.

——— 1 ———
Jeré Longman, "SOCCER; The Sports Bra Seen Round the World," *New York Times*, July 5, 2003, www.nytimes.com/2003/07/05/sports/soccer-the-sports-bra-seen-round-the-world.html.

——— 2 ———
Cathy Keen, "Jogbra: Providing Essential Support for Title Nine and Women Athletes," Smithsonian, December 11, 2014, americanhistory.si.edu/explore/stories/jogbra-providing-essential-support-title-nine-and-women-athletes.

FIG 288

FIG 289

287 Callisto Shorts and Pleat Skirt, Spring 1984

288 Lightweight Crew and Lightweight Pant, Spring 1984

289 Lightweight Turtleneck, Lady Spectrum II, and Women's Lightweight Pant, Spring 1984

FIG 290

IT'S A WOMAN'S PREROGATIVE TO CHANGE HER MIND.

FIG 291

And there's no better expression of that adage than cross-training.

Cross-training is a fitness regimen that may include running, weight training, aerobics, and any number

of court sports.

And Nike has the only women's shoe designed specifically for cross-training. One that can handle the demands of any number of sports without sacrificing

comfort or protection.

It's called the Air Trainer. And it features Nike-Air® cushioning. Cushioning that reduces the chance of shock-related injury to the bones, muscles, and tendons of the

foot and lower leg.

More importantly, Nike-Air never wears out.

But all this cushioning isn't at the expense of stability. A wide forefoot and a unique footframe hold your

foot in place during any and all lateral movements.

So get the Air Trainer Low. Or, for extra stability, the Air Trainer High. Then, start cross-training.

And change your mind

without changing your shoes.

Air Trainer High

Air Trainer Low

FIG 292

Multi-sport athlete Joanne Ernst features in this 1987 women's cross-training ad. At the time, she was the consummate female cross trainer, placing first in the 1985 Women's Division of the Ironman World Triathlon Championships in Hawaii, and third in the 1996 race. "We were launching cross-training to women exactly the same way we had done to men," longtime executive Deb Weekley told DNA. "There were very few women who exercised this way in 1988."

290 Airborne, Fall 1986

291 Air Trainer in "It's a Woman's Prerogative to Change Her Mind" featuring Joanne Ernst, 1987

292 Zoom 90 Airborne, Spring 1990

FIG 293

FIG 295

FIG 294

FIG 296

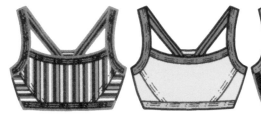

FIG 297

FIG 298

293 Aerobics Fitness Top, Holiday 1994

294 Swoosh Fitness Top, Spring 1994

295 Page from Cross-Training Collection Catalog, Fall 1989

296 Statement Microfiber Racer, Spring 1994

297 Summer Fitness Top, Spring 1993

298 Suspension Back Top (print), Spring 1993

FIG 299

▼

This Y-Back Cotton Lycra/Airborne Top was released in six colorways in 1988. It was among the first products to tout a "built-in support bra"—following behind the Running Airborne, which debuted in 1987. It wasn't until 1996, however, that Nike would use the word "bra" in a product name, with the arrival of the Fitness Bra Top. The pattern seen here, entitled "Motion Print," was also released on several other pieces of Nike apparel in the same season.

299 Y-Back Cotton/Lycra Airborne Top, 1988

300 Page from Women's Apparel Catalog, Spring 1990

**7HJ4 ELITE PRINT
ILLUSION LEOTARD**

**7HJ7 ELITE
PRINT WRAP LEOTARD**

7HJ0 ELITE SHEEN ILLUSION LEOTARD

7HJ1 ELITE SHEEN WRAP LEOTARD

**7HJ5 ELITE PRINT
MINI-AIRBORNE II**

**7HJ6 ELITE
PRINT AIRBORNE**

7HJ2 ELITE MINI-AIRBORNE II

7HJ3 ELITE SHEEN AIRBORNE

7DJ7 ELITE PRINT WRAP BRIEF

7DJ0 ELITE COTTON SHEEN WRAP BRIEF

7DJ1 ELITE COTTON SHEEN BACK SEAM SHORT

7DJ3 ELITE PRINT SHEEN BACK SEAM SHORT

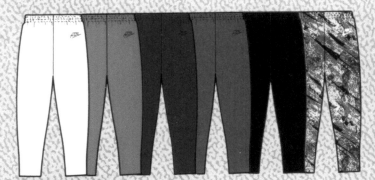

7DJ4 ELITE COTTON SHEEN BACK SEAM 3/4

7DJ5 ELITE PRINT SHEEN BACK SEAM 3/4

FIG 300

233

FIG 301

FIG 302

FIG 303

301 Page from Women's Apparel Catalog, Spring 1990

302 Page from Cross-Training Collection Catalog, Fall 1989

303 Page from Women's Apparel Catalog, Spring 1994

FIG 304

#1
#2
#3
#4
#5
#6

FIG 305

FIG 306

FIG 307

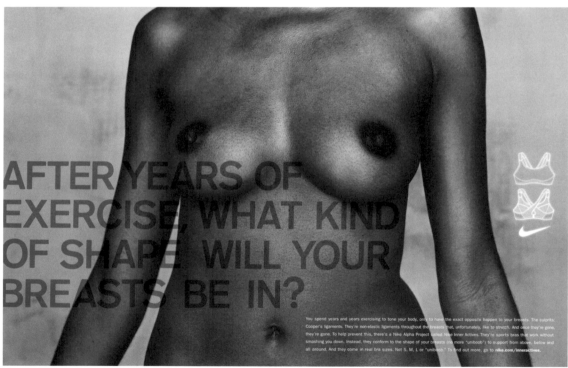

AFTER YEARS OF EXERCISE, WHAT KIND OF SHAPE WILL YOUR BREASTS BE IN?

You spend years and years exercising to tone your body, only to have the exact opposite happen to your breasts. The culprits: Cooper's ligaments. They're non-elastic ligaments throughout the breasts that, unfortunately, like to stretch. And once they're gone, they're gone. To help prevent this, there's a Nike Alpha Project called Nike Inner Actives. They're sports bras that work without smashing you down. Instead, they conform to the shape of your breasts (no more "uniboob") to support from above, below and all around. And they come in real bra sizes. Not S, M, L or "uniboob." To find out more, go to nike.com/inneractives.

▼

Nike launched its line of Inner Actives bras in September 1999 with a print campaign that placed the breasts front and center, sparking a new conversation about the importance of adequate support to breast health. Ads such as this one ran in addition to several more muted versions in which the nipples were obscured by hands, to be placed in magazines that were less comfortable with nudity, including *Shape* and *Women's Sports and Fitness*.

304 Logo size reference, Fall 2001

305 Bra Top, Fall 1994

306 Cover of Women's Apparel Catalog (detail), Fall 1994

307 Inner Actives bra in "After Years Of Exercise What Kind Of Shape Will Your Breasts Be In?", 1999

FIG 308

306

FIG 309

TRAINING FUNDAMENTALS

222023 BRA TOP

CONTENT: Body: 7.5 oz. 90% cotton/10% Lycra spandex jersey. Lining: 3 oz. 100% nylon circular knit.

PROFILE: Front lined short fitness top with scoop neck, elastic fabric main body, 1x1 elastic rib armholes and bottom hem, covered elastic at hem, embroidered Swoosh design trademark at center front chest.

WHOLESALE: $12.50 **SUGGESTED RETAIL:** $25.00

			S	M	L	XL			
050	Grey Heather/Grey Heather/(White) ☐	5/25							
100	White/White/(Black) ☐	5/25							
362	Moss/Tank/(Tank) ■	5/25							
386	Tank/Tank/(White) ☐	5/25							
425	Atlantic Blue/Obsidian/(Obsidian) ☐	5/25							
426	Atl Blue/Sargasso Print/Obsidian/(Columbia Blue) ☐	5/25							
448	Columbia Blue/Atlantic Blue/(Atlantic Blue) ☐	5/25							
451	Obsidian/Obsidian/(White) ☐	5/25							
456	Alpine Blue/Sargasso Print/Moss/(Moss) ☐	5/25							
655	Deep Red/Deep Red/(White) ☐	5/25							
010	Black/Black/(White) ☐	5/25							

FIG 310

FIG 311

FIG 312

LOOKS CAN *KILL*

Gabrielle Reece

FIG 313

313

Dubbed "the original athleisure cool girl" by US *Vogue*, volleyball star Gabrielle Reece was a mainstay of Nike advertising in the mid- to late-1990s. She was also the first female athlete with a signature Nike shoe; the Air Trainer Set was designed by Tinker Hatfield and launched in 1994.

313 "Looks Can Kill" Poster featuring Gabrielle Reece, 1993

Following spread:

314 "Questionnaire" completed by Gabrielle Reece, 1993

315 Bra Top, 1999

316 Short Colorblock Bra Top autographed by Gabrielle Reece, 1996

317 Aerobics Mini Fitness Top autographed by Jackie Joyner-Kersee, 1995

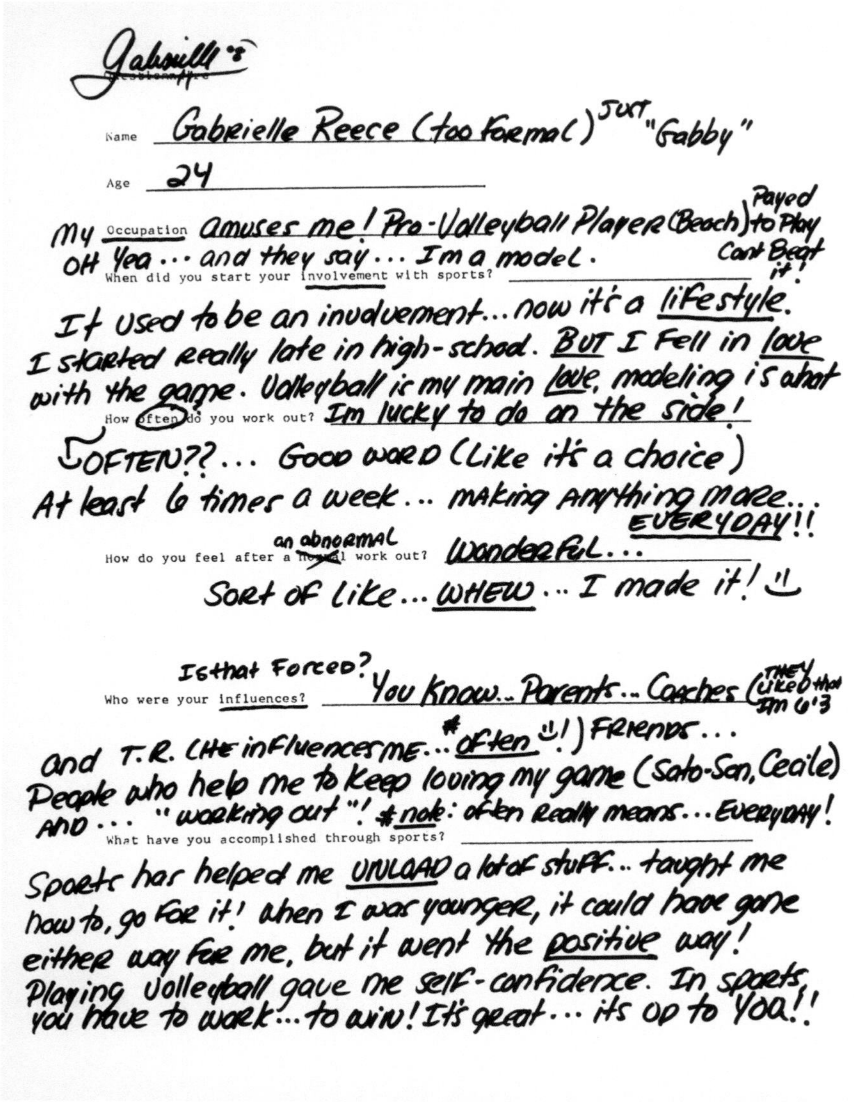

Gabrielle

Name _Gabrielle Reece (too Formal)_ JUST "Gabby"

Age _24_

My Occupation _amuses me! Pro-Volleyball Player (Beach)_ Payed to Play. Can't Beat it!
OH Yea... and they say... I'm a model.

When did you start your involvement with sports? _____

It used to be an involvement... now it's a *lifestyle*.
I started really late in high-school. _BUT_ I Fell in love
with the game. Volleyball is my main _love_, modeling is what

How often do you work out? _I'm lucky to do on the side!_

OFTEN??... Good word (Like it's a choice)
At least 6 times a week... making Anything more...
EVERYDAY!!

How do you feel after a ~~normal~~ an abnormal work out? _Wonderful..._
Sort of like... WHEW... I made it! :"

Is that FORCED?
Who were your influences? _You Know... Parents... Coaches_ (THEY LIKED that
I'm 6'3

and T.R. (He influences me... # _often_ :") FRIENDS...
People who help me to keep loving my game (Sato-San, Cecile)
AND... "*working out*"! # note: often really means... Everyday!

What have you accomplished through sports? _____

Sports has helped me _UNLOAD_ a lot of stuff... taught me
how to, go For it! When I was younger, it could have gone
either way for me, but it went the _positive_ way!
Playing Volleyball gave me self-confidence. In sports,
you have to work... to win! It's great... its up to YOU!!

FIG 314

FIG 315

240

FIG 316

FIG 317

FIG 318

318

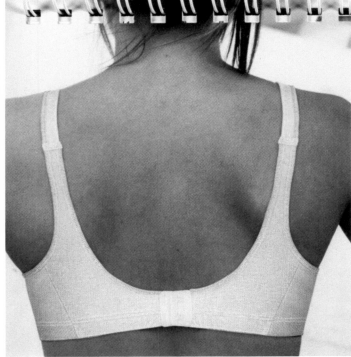

FIG 319

FIG 320

297014

FIG 321

225024

INTIMATES   324

FIG 322

FIG 323

FIG 324

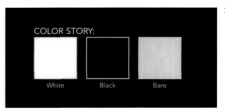

COLOR STORY:

White   Black   Bare

242

318 Inner Actives feature (detail), Fall 2000

319 Inner Actives feature (detail), Holiday 2000

320 Multisport Bra, Holiday 2004

321 Contour Walking Bra, Holiday 2004

322 Adjustable Pull-Over Bra, Holiday 2003

323 Performance Thong, Holiday 2000

324 Intimates Color Palette, Spring 2003

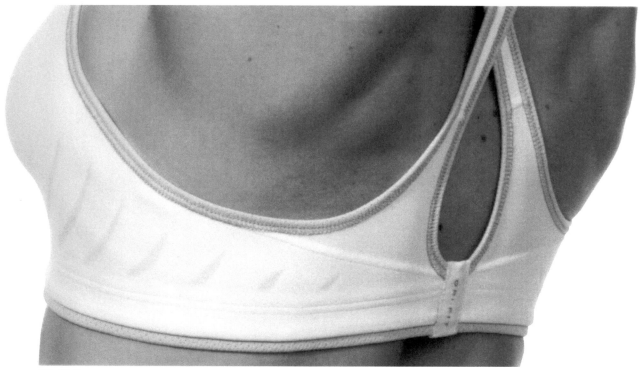

FIG 325

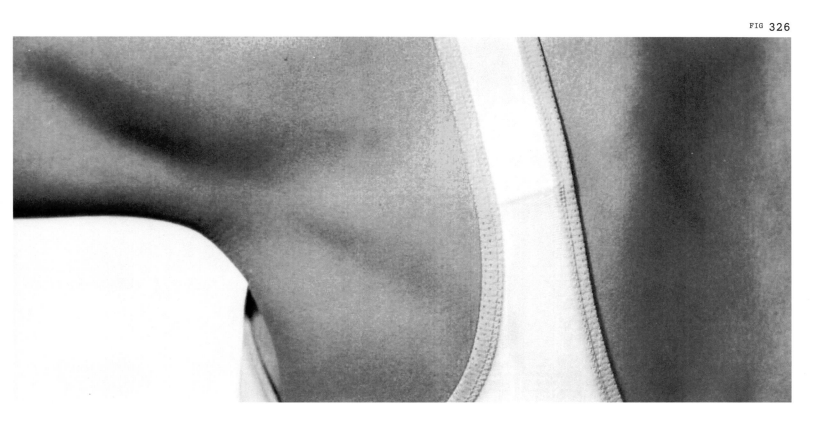

FIG 326

325 Inner Actives feature (detail), Spring 2001

326 Inner Actives feature (detail), Summer 2001

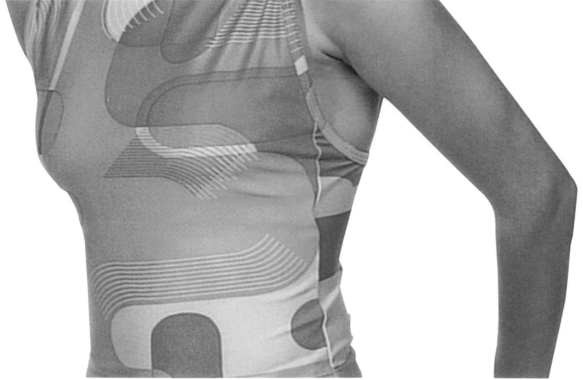

FIG 327

Hoop Orange | Hot Red

Light Hot Red | Light Neutral Grey

FIG 328

327 Tennis feature, Spring 2001

328 Color Palette, Spring 2001

329 Nike Revolutionary Support Bra, 2006

FIG 329

329

FINALLY, A RUNNING BRA DESIGNED FOR WOMEN.

Conventional wisdom states that a woman's breasts should be strapped down; that sports bras should limit all possible movement. In essence, what is being said is that the breasts should be eliminated; that women would work better if they were a bit more like men.

The Nike Revolutionary Support Bra is based on contemporary wisdom. Through a Natural Motion Engineering study, we found that controlling the breasts' interior is equally important as the exterior. With this in mind, we designed the bra to limit the entire breasts' movement, helping to keep important muscles and ligaments from stretching. We also widened the shoulder straps to allow for a better distribution of weight, and minimized the potential for chafing by using sonic sealing instead of stitching.

This all adds up to a bra that works with the way a woman works. Which should make sense, even to a man.

Beaverton, Oregon

FIG 330

The Revolutionary Support Bra was released in spring 2006, after a year and a half in development, and included four patent-pending technologies. The bra sought to maximize both performance and beauty through support, comfort, and a personal fit. It incorporated a 360-degree exoskeleton for compressive support, paired with an adjustable motion control strap that bifurcated the breasts. The Revolutionary Support Bra retailed for $70.00 USD and it was also available in white.

330 Revolutionary Support Bra ad, 2006

331 Nike Strength Bra, Spring 2008

332 Logo, Spring 2008

333 Core Bra Top, Spring 2009

334 New Dedication Short Airborne, Holiday 2009

335 Flirty Seamless Short Bra, Spring 2009

FIG 331

100   010

FIG 332

FIG 333

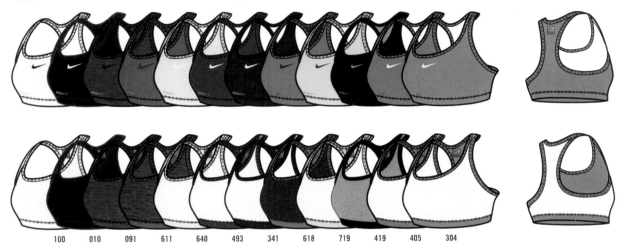

100 010 091 611 640 493 341 618 719 419 405 304

FIG 334

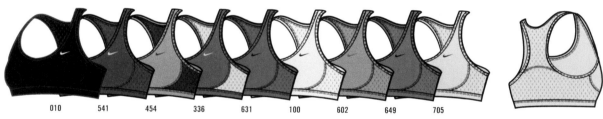

010 541 454 336 631 100 602 649 705

FIG 335

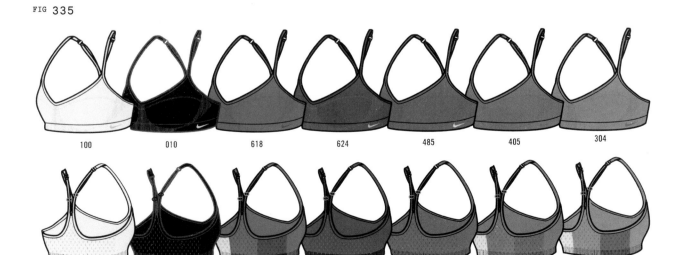

100   010   618   624   485   405   304

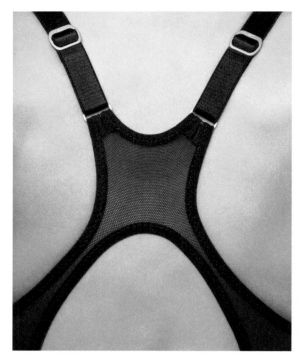

FIG 336

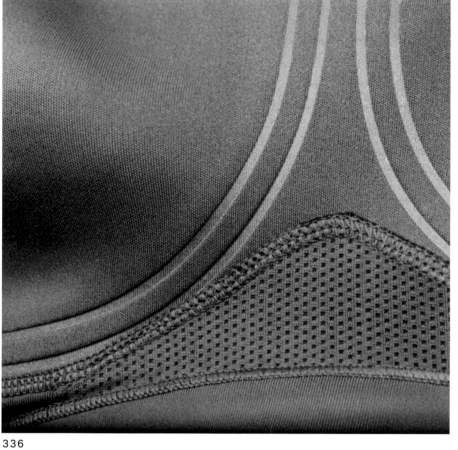

336

336

FIG 337

VICTORY SUPPORT SYSTEM

FIG 338

FIG 339

LEAD/FLOW 1

GERANIUM

LEGION RED

*LASER CRIMSON

TURBO GREEN

NIGHT SHADE

NEUTRALS

BLACK

WHITE

ANTHRACITE

*VOLT

BASE GREY

MEDIUM BASE GREY

DARK BASE GREY

SEASPRAY

MICA GREEN

DARK MICA GREEN

LEAD/FLOW 2

*ATOMIC MANGO

KUMQUAT

*LASER CRIMSON

GERANIUM

LEGION RED

FIG 340

*TURBO GREEN

*LT LUCID GREEN

*VOLT

*BRIGHT GRAPE

*LASER CRIMSON

*TURBO GREEN

*LT LUCID GREEN

*ATOMIC MANGO

BLACK

WHITE

*ATOMIC MANGO

KUMQUAT

FIG 341

nike.com/women

250

FIG 342

FIG 343

343 Nike Pro Rival Dalmation Bra, 2015

344 NRG Bra, 2019

345 Nike Indy Lightweight Support Performance JDI Bra, 2018

FIG 344

FIG 345

FIG 348

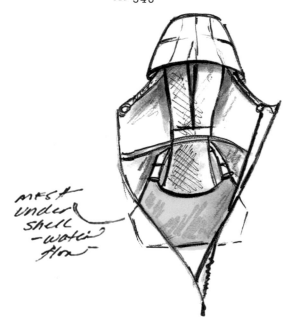

FIG 346

346

FIG 347

346 Alate Sports Bra

347 Nike (M) Launch featuring Perri Edwards, 2020

348 Victory Swim Collection sketches, 2019

349 Victory Swim campaign, 2019

348

FIG 349

Handwritten annotations on figure:
- COATED ZIPPER
- MESH VENT BACK NECK
- HAIR POUCH "HAIR management" (COIFFURE)
- iridescent piping 17 FLAMES PIXEL beauty
- comfort fold over & elastic = less irritation
- MESH BRA FRAME "CONFIDENCE" & perforated cups
- ZIPPER END COVER
- adjustable bra straps: "FIT"
- iridescent cuffs
- mesh insets = waterflow
- high waistband w/ internal mesh = control comfort secure
- zip pocket

In 2019 Nike released the Victory Swim Collection, combining performance apparel and modest swimwear for women requiring full coverage and a full range of motion in a lightweight, quick-drying fabric. The silhouettes were simple: the Hijab, the Tunic Top, and the Swim Leggings, all designed in black and cut to sit away from the body. But extensive research conducted in collaboration with hijabi and modest athletes revealed a need for aesthetic appeal beneath the outer layers, too. An adjustable perforated bra was built into the tunic, quick draining and quick drying, while also providing support in the water. It was also pearlescent—purposeful, but beautiful.

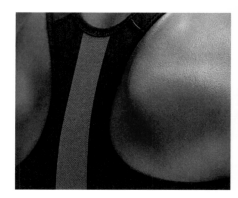

350

FIG 350

350

FIG 351

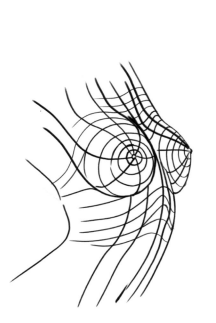

FIG 352

FIG 353

▼

In the 2010s Flyknit technology developed for footwear design presented new possibilities for the bra. The FE/NOM Flyknit Bra was made from a soft spandex yarn woven to fit the form of the body. Two single-layer panels, assembled without seams, replace the up to 41 individual pieces that comprise a traditional sports bra. The FE/NOM combined compression with encapsulation, softness with comfort, and weighed around 30% less than other sports bras had to date. It also carried color excellently: at the 2019 World Cup, every national team's kit included a coordinating FE/NOM bra.

350 FE/NOM Flyknit Bra, 2019

351 FE/NOM Flyknit Bra campaign, 2019

352 FE/NOM Flyknit Bra sketch

353 Nike FE/NOM Flyknit Bra, 2017

August 24, 2023. Budapest, Hungary.

Anna Cockrell takes a minute's rest after competing in the women's 400-meter hurdles final during the World Athletics Championships.

January 15, 2024. Melbourne, Australia.

Naomi Osaka wears an iridescent snakeskin look to compete in the first round of the Australian Open—her first Slam back in the game after giving birth to her daughter.

May 3, 2019. Doha, Qatar.

Caster Semenya looks up before taking to the track during the IAAF Diamond League.

ATHLETE: ANNA COCKRELL   SUBJECT: BREATHING

BIOGRAPHY: Anna Cockrell is an American track and field athlete who competes in the
100- and 400-meter hurdles, and the 4×400-meter sprint. She was born in 1997
in California, USA.

The sports bra is the most foundational piece for me, because being in touch with my breathing is really important.

I quickly learned that the longline bras that come down to your rib cage are an absolute no, never, for me.

I feel suffocated in them.

I'm almost always in a Swoosh bra, or a light Indy bra.

I have a regular black one that's my old faithful—

it's probably lost some of its elastic; it's time to get a new one.

My training partners make fun of me; they say they know when it's getting hard and I'm trying to lock in because

I'll roll the waistband of my shorts down.

I need my whole stomach out—I need full diaphragm engagement to breathe.

I need to feel that expansion.

ATHLETE: NAOMI OSAKA

SUBJECT: SNAKESKIN

I've always felt like my personal style gives me power, like I can dress up and become a different person.

Now I'm in a transition.

Becoming a mother has shifted my style, in that I want to experiment more.

My outfit for this Australian Open meant a lot to me, mainly because it was my first Slam back [since giving birth to my daughter].

I've always thought it would be beautiful to play in a reflective snakeskin outfit.

Snakes can be seen as a bad omen, but some are reflective, some are beautiful.

And they shed their skin.

ATHLETE: CASTER SEMENYA

SUBJECT: THE CHAIN

BIOGRAPHY: Caster Semenya is a South African middle-distance runner who competes in the
400-, 4×400-, 800-, and 1500-meter races. She was born in 1991 in Ga-Masehlong,
South Africa.

There are some pieces that define my performance.

I cannot run without my chain.

It gives me rhythm, because when I run it bounces up and down—bam, bam, bam, bam—

and it sets the pace.

My cornrows need to look on point, to say, 'I'm ready.'

I never forget my earrings, either.

In my diamonds, I look cool.

Because I'm a diamond, you know?

ATHLETE: MEGAN RAPINOE

SUBJECT: DYEING HER HAIR

BIOGRAPHY: Megan Rapinoe is an American football player. She
               was born in 1985 in California, USA.

When your hair is this short and blonde, it really doesn't matter what the colors are, you can throw anything in there.

It's just another way to express yourself.

Sometimes it's a tool of resistance, or bucking up against authority, or an expression of being queer.

And sometimes it's just not that big of a deal.

It is so important to know that you can do that if you want to.

As a woman, and especially as a gay woman, I didn't have that growing up.

It tells kids that things they don't normally see are possible.

Like, this is what I like to do; you can do whatever you want.

That is something I think about—being gay and being able to speak out on things—and I saw it reflected back too.

You put any sort of person who doesn't fit into a box on the world stage, and that's powerful.

You don't have to look the same as everybody else in order to be successful.

ATHLETE: CASTER SEMENYA

SUBJECT: THE BODYSUIT

When I run, I feel free, fearless.

Supernatural.

I'm in a zone of my own.

I always feel powerful in a bodysuit, because it fits.

It's tight; it portrays power.

I'm never under any distress. I can be myself, go out and perform, and I perform my best.

If I could only keep one thing from all the sportswear I own, I'd keep my bodysuit.

I can go back to every race that I've ever run in a bodysuit, and I've never lost.

When I die I'll say, 'Bury me in that bodysuit!'

I have a lot of memories in my bodysuit.

Records I've broken.

It shows the power I have, how strong a human being I am.

the   body:

michelle millar fisher

owned

In Sport England's *This Girl Can* 2017 campaign video—one of four in a series that aimed to encourage female participation in sport—Maya Angelou's voice (taken from a recording) drips deliciously over a montage of women and girls who gyrate, grunt, heave, and whoop their way through physical activities.[1] The poet reads verses from her paean to positive self-appreciation, "Phenomenal Woman" (1978), to frame these people of all ages and abilities. Their authentic joy, even through exertion and exhaustion, is infectious.

The medley captures scenarios where a personal best is an attitude, not a stopwatch reading. Participants aren't wearing any fancy uniforms. In fact, they warm up in leggings that long ago lost their stretch, snap cheap goggles to their heads as they prep their aging bodies for the pool, and wear bright yellow boxing gloves alongside workaday hijabs. Far from the biology of their bodies or the social constructions of their gender being impediments, a series of battles to be fought before they get mobile, they portray active womanhood as an expansive force to be reckoned with. Every time I watch them, I am inspired to lace up my own ratty running shoes and head outside.

Contrarily for an essay on women and the designs they don while active, these phenomenal, ordinary women are a testament to the truth that it isn't what we wear when we exercise that is significant. Instead, what counts is the way we assert agency by moving our bodies and reveling in the feelings produced as our heart rates rise. As Angelou reminds us, "It's in the reach of my arms / The span of my hips / The stride of my step / The curl of my lips / I'm a woman / Phenomenally."

Amen.

Except that one usually doesn't turn up at the gym, court, or competition naked, and so while we could—and I would—argue that what we wear is secondary to how we feel when we exercise, sports garments can make, and have made, a difference to this equation. What women wear inside and on their bodies when they play sports becomes imprinted with blood, sweat, tears, pee, and other excretions of their exertion. Because of that, such designs often significantly impact their sense of control and comfort. These needs change and evolve just as all bodies do, with age and experience.

Such design thus enables those who identify as women to feel ownership over their wildly divergent bodies through arcs that, for each of them, may or may not include adolescence, menstruation, injury, pregnancy, motherhood, disability, or menopause. The history of how such ownership has been negotiated is checkered. In the world of sport, the female body is not just shaped by practice laps or a well-fitted sports bra. It is a socially constructed site where ideas about gender, race, sexuality, and class are rehearsed and reinforced.[2] In this scenario, the body is a porous and political frontier over which women have had to—and continue to—fight to raise their own flags. And raise them they do. Again and again, over finish lines and personal bests and long-held, hard-fought dreams.

[1] Throughout this essay I intend the term woman to include anyone who identifies with this moniker.

[2] Martha H. Verbrugge, "Gender, Science & Fitness: Perspectives on Women's Exercise in the United States in the 20th Century," *Health and History* 4, no. 1 (2002): 54.

Stories of women's bodies in sports aren't ever easy or linear, but this makes them all the more inspiring—and sometimes maddening. In telling them, we map a powerful stage for new generations of phenomenal women and girls, claim ownership of both our bodies and our narratives, and retain the same sense of wonder at what we can achieve as the movers and shakers profiled in the Sport England campaign. This essay explores these truths.

We can't start this story without some context for why women in sports have had an uphill battle to retain their agency and autonomy. If modern sports evolved in the nineteenth century as a way to regulate, organize, and rationalize the body in tandem with the advent of capitalism and industrialization, a century later, fitness maven Jane Fonda gave this process its perfect maxim. "Exercise," she noted provocatively, "teaches you the pleasure of discipline."[3] (She later refined this to the pithier "Discipline is liberation!") Her videos, the first of which debuted in 1982, held up a mirror to the concurrent, frenetic rise of fitness clubs, home exercise media, and personal trainers. Their disciplinary message had a primary recipient: women. Fonda's pelvic thrusts propagated the idea that the female body was a project to be carefully tended through consumption—of the "right" foods in the "right" amounts, of workout clothes that accentuated a svelte form, and of regimented workouts just like hers.

We may never know if Fonda read the work of French philosopher Michel Foucault, who found contemporaneous fame in his own more esoteric way with texts such as *Discipline and Punish* (1975). However, her exercise videos epitomized his conjecture that to discipline was to enact power, a means to render bodies docile through self-surveillance and thus pliable for a society whose plans for them were as cogs in a larger industrial machine. While his scholarship interrogated the operations of organizations such as the modern army, school, and hospital, in his description of mustering "biopower" through "movements, gestures, attitudes, rapidity," and his assertion that "the only truly important ceremony is that of exercise," one need only squint and imagine him thinking of Jane Fonda's workout tapes too.[4]

Those who shimmied along in their living rooms were told they were taking control of their bodies and, by extension, their destinies. But au contraire. Their bodies were not their own. They were instead molded by the same media and marketers who sold them all the other gadgets and gizmos of the modern home that promised to save them labor—and rarely did. The history of twentieth-century advertising was built on a model where predominantly male retailers and marketers told those who held household spending power—the majority of whom were women—what to aspire to and the products that would get them there.

Called fitness and packaged as a leisure activity, physical activity was swept into this equation. Twenty-four workout videos followed Fonda's first, generating $17 million USD in sales, an insatiable demand for at-home VHS players, and a way to link fitness to appearance, and appearance to sex appeal. This last ingredient was expressed narrowly in the form of the slim, white, premenopausal, able-bodied women who populated Fonda's classes and whose bodies fit the Goldilocks paradigm: not too hard, not too soft, just pliant enough to consume.[5]

I write this and then check in with this book's author, Maisie. "Too much of a downer?" I ask. We'd initially agreed on the essay focusing on women's empowerment. She reads, checks the footnotes, and tilts her head in thought. "It's truthful," she says. We agree that's not just a good but a necessary place to start.

It was no coincidence that Sport England chose an emotive ad campaign to encourage women to exercise rather than, say, free gym memberships for all. They used mass media because they understood its dominant role—and thus its potential to undo what one academic calls the "hegemonic masculinity and emphasized femininity"[6] present in sports culture, where men's "power and performance" are juxtaposed with women's "pleasure and participation."[7] This stereotype has its roots where patriarchy and capitalism meet women's medical history. Its first operation is to essentialize womanhood via binary sex characteristics and then indelibly tie this to a wider social desire to control a perceived capacity for biological reproduction and care work.

Nineteenth-century physicians offered a flawed logic that women were forever "victims of their reproductive apparatus."[8] Such quack science was once widely propagated, articulating a belief in menstruation as a form of recurrent disability that cast those who experienced it as "both the weaker and a periodically weakened sex."[9] Lo and behold, a period became automatic grounds to show women the door during gym class.

Examples of similar intellectual and scientific poverty made it from the doctor's office into early mass media, lending weight to gendered limits that became imbricated in sport. At the advent of basketball in the late nineteenth century, for example, special rules determined restrictive on-court zones for female players, who could only bounce the ball once before passing in order not to dislodge their uterus or faint from overexertion. Popular magazines reinforced such absurd, unsubstantiated ideas, with *Harper's Bazaar* wondering, "Are athletics a menace to motherhood?" in 1912 and, seventy-five years later, still asking, "Can Sports Make You Sterile?"[10]

Far from yesterday's news, this lunacy persisted—which is why it's important to spell it out in a book like this, which looks at sportswomen now. A similar argument was made as recently as the 2014 Sochi Winter Olympics in Russia to dissuade the inclusion of women in the ski-jumping competition without ever asking the participants themselves how they prioritized their reproductive and sporting freedoms.[11]

In the nineteenth and twentieth centuries, public discourse also frequently coded female participation in sports as synonymous with queer sexuality and a refusal of socially mandated, subservient, and heteronormative care roles for women. To wit, a 1934 *Literary Digest* writer warned that girls who were encouraged to undertake physical education "might find it difficult to attract the most worthy fathers for their children."[12] Anything

---

— 3 —

The scholar Pam A. Sailors punctures the hegemony of such experiences by drawing physical activities from the DIY margins to center stage—for example roller derbies, for which participants not only devise their own uniforms but take great pride and pleasure in personalizing them.

— 4 —

Michel Foucault, "Docile Bodies," in *Discipline and Punish* (New York: Vintage Books, 1975), 137. See also Jen Pylypa, "Power and Bodily Practice: Applying the Work of Foucault to an Anthropology of the Body," *Arizona Anthropologist* 13 (1998): 21–36.

— 5 —

Pam R. Sailors, Sarah Teetzel, and Charlene Weaving, "Core Workout: A Feminist Critique of Definitions, Hyperfemininity, and the Medicalization of Fitness," *International Journal of Feminist Approaches to Bioethics* 9, no. 2 (2016): 53.

— 6 —

Timothy J. Curry, Paula A. Arriagada, and Benjamin Cornwell, "Images of Sport in Popular Non-Sport Magazines: Power and Performance versus Pleasure and Participation," *Sociological Perspectives* 45, no. 4 (Winter 2002), 397.

— 7 —

Between 1957 and 1989, coverage of women in sport actually *declined*, from 15 percent in the 1950s to between 4 and 6 percent in the three decades that followed, and when gender meets other intersectional identities such as race, the wedge gets even sharper. Jo Ann M. Buysse and Melissa Sheridan Embser-Herbert, "Constructions of Gender in Sport: An Analysis of Intercollegiate Media Guide Cover Photographs," *Gender and Society* 18, no. 1 (February 2004), 68. See also: Akilah R. Carter-Francique and F. Michelle Richardson, "Controlling Media, Controlling Access," *Race, Gender & Class* 23, no. 1–2, 7–33.

— 8 —

Verbrugge, "Gender, Science & Fitness," (2002): 53.

Their goal was to reorient the conversation about who owned women's bodies:

women themselves.

different was not only seen as personally deviant but as a destabilizing disruption to the social imperative of population replenishment.

This policing of gender and sexuality in women's sports is sensitively taken up by Lindsay Pieper in her excellent 2016 history *Sex Testing*. There, she details the ignominy and invasion experienced by athletes after testing for genital and chromosomal makeup became enshrined in the late 1960s. The first attempt by the International Federation in 1966 involved a humiliating parade of naked female athletes before a panel of male doctors. In 1985, shocked to learn she had XY chromosomes, Spanish hurdler María José Martínez-Patiño demanded further testing, an experience that, when combined with media hounding over leaked medical records, she likened to rape.[13] The Spaniard's story—echoed decades later in the experiences of one of her countrywomen in a forced kiss at the 2023 Women's World Cup trophy ceremony—is a stark reminder that celebrating women's sporting power means bearing witness to all of the blood, sweat, and tears they shed, not just those that make for acceptable or aspirational reading.

Even much later, when social attitudes might have been expected to have changed in tandem with seismic shifts to legislation around women in sport (not least Title IX[14]), new generations of female athletes were still on the receiving end of messages about keeping menstruation, motherhood, or menopause invisible unless a sporting body or abusive coach or doctor wanted to invade their privacy—and then all bets were off, including a right to personal safety. This was the status quo for people more usually spoken for, to, or about rather than listened to in sport.[15]

Yet for all these external conflicts, omissions, and claims of ownership over the female body, women have not been passive victims of this sports history. Quite the opposite. In the last generation in particular, increasingly frustrated with a field that has overlooked or denied their needs, they have become the authors and inventors of new paradigms. They have engaged with sports design as stakeholders, investors, designers, or informed consumers. Superstar athletes with their own lines and platforms might immediately spring to mind. However, I think of designs that shatter taboos with the sustained, understated persistence of a distance runner, like the supple silicone Reia prolapse pessary that inserts into the vagina in order to keep descending organs in check. Pelvic prolapse is an experience that 50 percent of people with uteruses will have at some stage, and one that, alongside related issues such as urinary incontinence, is often exacerbated by sports. An all-female design team took up the challenge in 2019 after no design typology upgrade had been attempted since 1938. It is but one example of the ways in which women—in the most expansive definition of that word—are owning their own experiences and pursuing the exhilaration of moving their bodies in whatever sport that moves them.

I was an avid reader of *Total Sport* magazine as a kid, which was the UK's answer to *Sports Illustrated*. I thought of it as a way to learn outside the lines of my rural Scottish education. In its pages I found stories and images from

---

13

S. C. Cornell, "Who Gets to Play in Women's Leagues," *New Yorker*, December 2, 2023.

9

Patricia Vertinsky, "Exercise, Physical Capability, and the Eternally Wounded Woman in Late Nineteenth Century North America," *Journal of Sport History* 14, no. 1 (1987): 9.

10

Verbrugge, "Gender, Science & Fitness," (2002): 52.

11

Francisco Valdes, "Queers, Sissies, Dykes, and Tomboys: Deconstructing the Conflation of 'Sex,' 'Gender,' and 'Sexual Orientation' in Euro-American Law and Society," *California Law Review* 83, no. 1 (1995): 52.

12

Susan K. Cahn, "From the 'Muscle Moll' to the 'Butch' Ballplayer: Mannishness, Lesbianism, and Homophobia in U.S. Women's Sport," *Feminist Studies* 19, no. 2 (Summer 1993): 343.

14

Title IX of the 1972 Education Amendments to the Constitution states that "No person in the United States shall, on the basis of sex, be excluded from participation in, be denied the benefits of, or be subjected to discrimination under any educational program or activity receiving federal assistance."

15

Sports media, from intercollegiate press departments to the cover of *Sports Illustrated*, follows the same stereotyped gender depictions as in the wider popular press where men dominate coverage with stories of success. See Jo Ann M. Buysse et al., "Constructions of Gender in Sport," (February 2004).

around the world and across intersections, from the civil rights movement embodied by the Black Power salute at the 1968 Mexico City Olympics to critiques of sports leveraged for nation-building. But today, as I reread *Total Sport* issues from the 1990s, the messages I understood then hit differently now as I see covers and features with one major commonality: the majority of them centered around men.

In 1990, just as I became an impressionable, *Total Sport*–obsessed teen in the Scottish Borders, a team of women creatives at the Portland, Oregon, ad agency Wieden+Kennedy made one of the first concerted efforts to address the skewed gender narratives I was swallowing. Working together, they demonstrated that claiming joy, wonder, and power for professional and amateur athletes alike was a team sport. Their client—and the impetus for such an odyssey—was Nike. Like every other major sports retailer, Nike had some work to do in the realm of gender equality. Their goal was to reorient the conversation about who owned women's bodies: women themselves. Art director Charlotte Moore and her colleague, copywriting magician Janet Champ, locked themselves in a conference room and waded through women's magazines, a process they found "so disgusting . . . [that] we made a list of what made us sick. . . . In lieu of working out, we wrote out feelings."[16] As Moore put it, "Women's magazines were full of ways to 'fix' ourselves. . . . Nobody suggested you try something that you could do for free. Nobody used photographs of women over eighteen."[17]

In an industry that had often defaulted to the "shrink it and pink it" model, Nike's first women's campaign, "List," in the fall of 1990 enumerated the countless products women were usually cautioned to use to artificially mold their bodies into acceptable shape: "your push-up bra . . . your control-top pantyhose . . . your black anything." Without showing any products, the female creative team countered this prescriptive list with a simple alternative: "self-support." A subsequent print campaign juxtaposed the social expectation that women prioritize finding a significant other with the assertion that, through physical activity, "you [become] significant to yourself." They went on to disseminate similar messages over the next seven years, highlighting grit and community over product every time. It was the model Sport England would use thirty years later to remind women of their collective and individual power to move.

Champ, Moore, and a later art director, Rachel Manganiello, were often the only women in the room at pitch meetings with Nike executives. Their budgets were usually far less than for campaigns aimed at men in sports. And so, fueled by their own experiences, they broke barriers in their workplace as they built ads designed to do the same for women in the wider world. Female audiences responded, calling and writing in to affirm that finally they felt seen by a company that had so long dominated the conversation without offering them a seat at the table.

While Nike did eventually sign well-known female athletes for some subsequent campaigns, it was the unknown narrators who were always the most powerful. In Nike's 1995 "If You Let Me Play" television campaign, which was scripted using research from the Women's Sports Foundation, girls and young women offered statistics directly to the camera: "If you let me play, I will suffer less depression. If you let me play, I will be 60 percent less likely to get breast cancer. If you let me play, I will be more likely to leave a man who beats me. If you let me play, I will be less likely to get pregnant before I want to. I will learn what it means to be strong. If you let me play sports."

As I watched, I couldn't help but think of the sports hijab—and not just the product itself but the culture built around it. In 2001 a recent graduate of the Design Academy Eindhoven in the Netherlands, Cindy van den Bremen, founded the first sports hijab company in the world, Capsters. She saw a growing Muslim population driven by immigration from former colonies and economic migration, but there was a failure to include women and girls in sports because the hijab was seen as a safety concern and/or an affront to secularism. Van den Bremen used Velcro for a quick-release hijab design and set a new benchmark for inclusion in the field. But in my eyes, the tipping point truly occurred a few years later when a Muslim competitor became not only the consumer but also the producer of what they needed for safe participation.

I will never forget the roar of delight as fencer Ibtihaj Muhammad—the first American Olympian to compete in a hijab—medaled at the 2016 Rio Olympics. Two years earlier, she had founded the modest fashion line Louella, producing the headgear she wore that day. While Nike went on to launch its own version of the sports hijab in 2017, their most important contribution was made decades earlier by Moore, Champ, and their team, who fostered a new standard around the culture of women in sport. They weren't unaware that what one wore counted—they knew their jobs, after all—but they knew it was nothing without feeling "that rush you get, that joy of having your body do things you never thought it was capable of."[18]

Fact-checking this section with Maisie and Nike's senior director of corporate narrative communications, Nicholas Schonberger, we talked about the potency of these stories and the ways in which they demonstrate a consistent movement forward, despite hurdles. I think back to the birthing mother in the Sport England campaign, straining against a rolled-up towel as she pushes new life into the world. It's no coincidence that in the edit, Maya Angelou's voice drawls the most powerful descriptor in her poem—phenomenally—over that image. Like that mother, an athlete's grit and determination and exertion and endurance and pain are inextricably linked to her arms raised in relief and wonder when she finally makes it over the finish line. To tell a truthful story of women's bodies in sports is only possible if this bittersweet synthesis, this hybrid of triumph and adversity, is acknowledged.

What does it mean today to have body autonomy or to "own" one's own body? Who gets to have this autonomy? For better and for worse, what we design to use as we play sports shapes the answers to these questions in ways that matter. So often, when we think of these designs, our imaginations

— 16 —

Jean M. Grow and Joyce M. Wolburg, "Selling Truth: How Nike's Advertising to Women Claimed a Contested Reality," *Advertising & Society Review* 7, no. 2 (2006).

— 17 —

Jean M. Grow, "Stories of Community: The First Decade of Nike Women's Advertising," *Proceedings of the American Academy of Advertising*, 2005, 10.

— 18 —

Jean M. Grow, "The Gender of Branding: Early Nike Women's Advertising a Feminist Antenarrative," *Women's Studies in Communication* 31, no. 3 (2009): 329.

I am alive, I am alive, I am *alive*.

are dominated by what we can most immediately see or what we have been most heavily sold. But for people who have the biological apparatus coded as female, or the socially constructed identity of a woman, the designs that help us feel most in control of our bodies and personhood are often much less visible. It's the role of language, beliefs, and the stories we tell ourselves and others that counts the most.

Six years ago, after my beloved mother died, I started running. I had never run further than for the train, but I needed to move my body to let out the grief. I ran through the streets of Glasgow like a madwoman—out of breath, weeping, snot plastered across my face. After a few months I decided I would run a marathon to mark a year without my mum, by which point I lived in Philadelphia. And so, one crisp and cold Saturday morning in November, I set off with thousands of other people in that city. I hadn't told anyone what I was going to do, and didn't let my husband come watch. It was just for me and her. I wore a pair of woolen gloves she'd given me the year before, and a pair of Nikes gifted to me by a friend around the same time.

As I made it through those hours, I thought of my last minutes with her a year earlier, and the rhythm of my running became a quasi-religious mantra that repeated in my mind mile after mile: I am alive, I am alive, I am *alive*. As I passed the finish line, I looked down at my body. It felt like a kind of magic that my blood still circulated while hers did not, and yet I was reminded that every cell of it had been built by her body thirty-six years earlier. It was her last gift to me, this view of my phenomenal, ordinary body fueled by the abiding message that she'd taught me from birth: your body is your own; don't let anyone tell you otherwise.

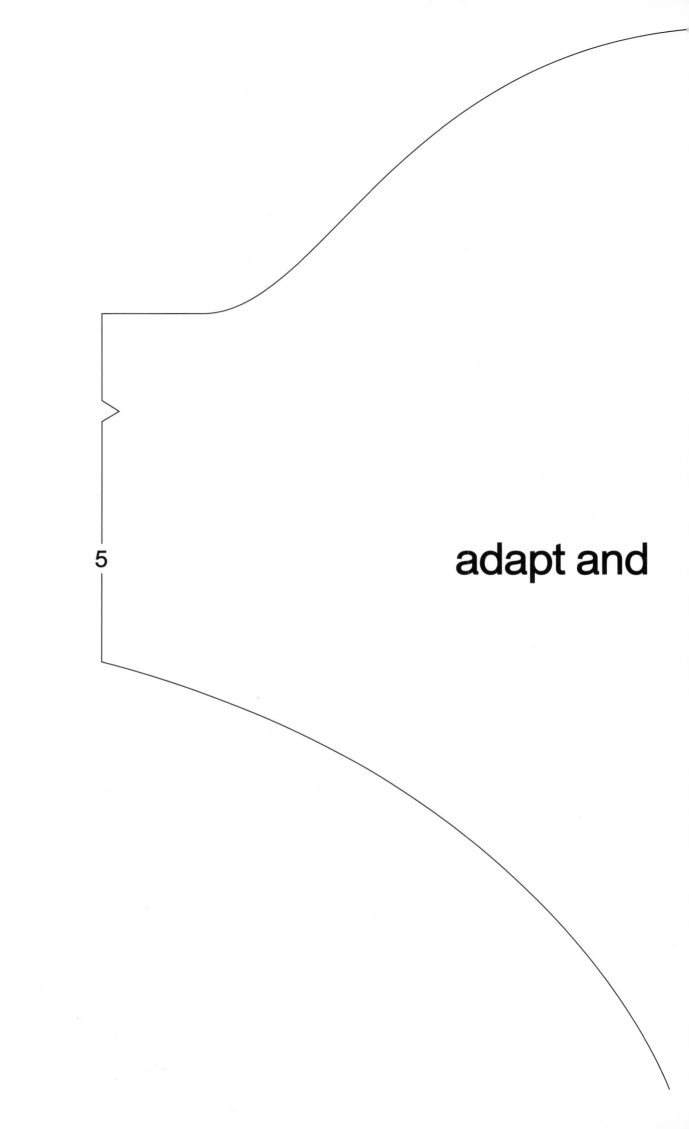

5

adapt and

evolve

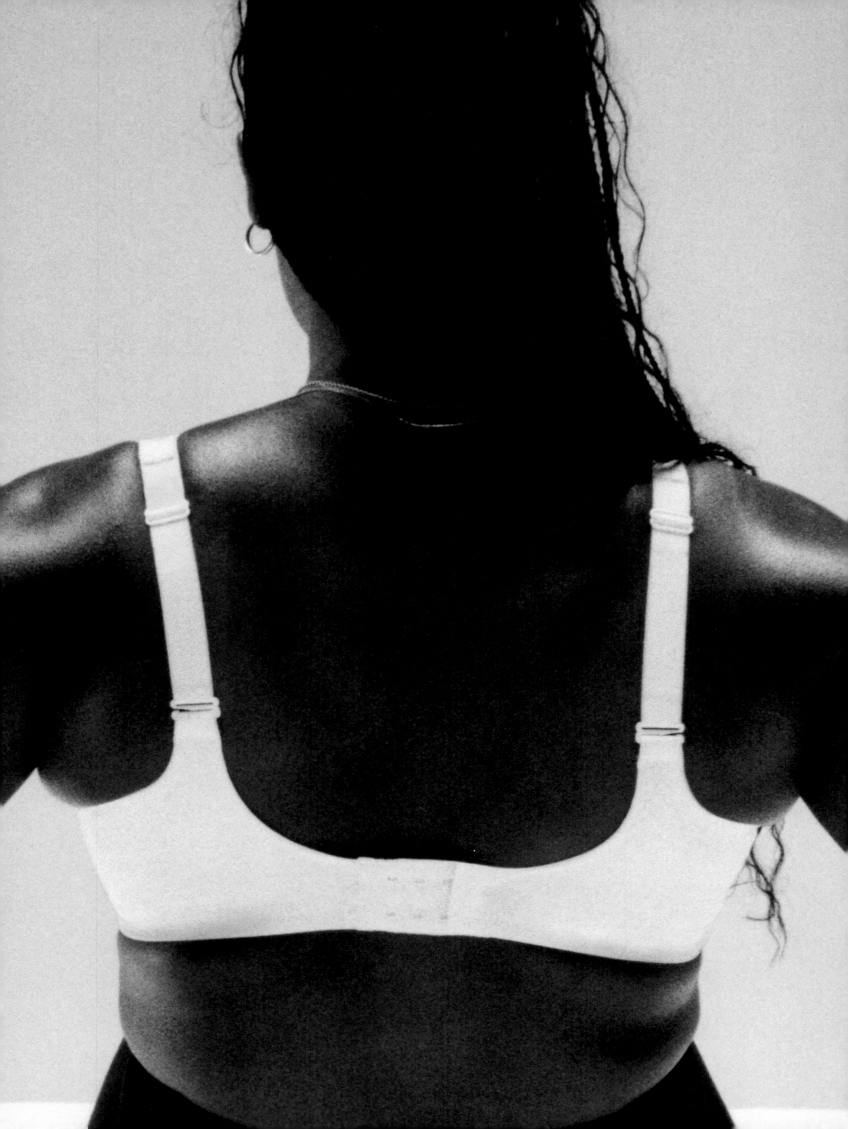

Women are

and they're dete

on the field,

mined to level it.

shorts

FIG 354

FIG 355

354

There are two refrains that reverberate through any conversation about the history of women's sports apparel, both at Nike and beyond. The first, "Shrink it and Pink it," refers to the time-honored practice of taking a men's garment and reproducing it in a smaller size range, in a color palette of pinks, purples, turquoises, and the like. The second, even less generous to female athletes, speaks for itself: "She wore a men's small."

Women can wear a men's small, of course—just as they can wear a men's medium, large, or extra large if they choose. But to choose, there must first be a choice, and historically the lack thereof has forced female athletes, professional and otherwise, into ill-fitting and ill-equipped garments, if not out of sport altogether. This oversight has become the backbone of women's athletic apparel, insofar as everything else pushes against it and builds upon it.

Women's shorts are not a simple garment. Like all high-performing pieces, they require a perfect fit across the full size range and cross-section of body shapes, with accommodations made for support, comfort, and functionality. Among the concerns: waistband, inseam length, fit to the body, and thigh chafe. Pockets are of key importance, with cases made fervently both for and against. Also at the forefront of consideration are weatherproofing and leak-proofing, style, and safety (shorts are regularly worn under skirts or dresses as an additional layer of security). The requirements shift across categories—football, basketball, yoga, tennis, volleyball, and so on. Everyday wear has its own particular parameters, and a contemporary wearer might choose shorts equally for running an errand or for running a 10K.

When Nike was founded by Bill Bowerman and Phil Knight in 1964 under the name Blue Ribbon Sports, it was not particularly concerned with apparel, men's or women's. And yet Nike-branded clothing played a part in some of the most important women's sporting milestones around the world. Take the 1979 Boston Marathon, at which the women's leaderboard was topped by twenty-one-year-old Bowdoin College senior Joan Benoit Samuelson, who achieved a finish time of 2:35:15, setting a new American record. She was not yet a Nike athlete, but she won wearing Nike Elite sneakers and Nike running shorts. Note that Nike did not yet manufacture women's running shorts; Joan Benoit Samuelson broke the women's world record wearing, presumably, a men's small.

354

FIG 356

FIG 357

ATHLETICS WEST

FIG 358

FIG 359

In 1977 Phil Knight and Geoff Hollister came together with elite high school coach Harry Johnson to launch Athletics West, the country's first corporate-sponsored, post-collegiate running club. It was created to give US athletes graduating from college the support and coaching required to take them to the next level, and in so doing, bring the US up to scratch with their European counterparts. The club's female athletes included Joan Benoit Samuelson and Mary Decker Slaney, both of whom are considered among the greatest female runners.

354 "Buy a Poster, Help an Athlete" Ad featuring Henry Rono (detail), 1979

355 Nike Running Shorts, 1978

356 Joan Benoit finishes the Boston Marathon, 1979

357 Athletics West Hang Tag, 1985

358 Spree Shorts, 1982

359 Relay Shorts, Spring 1983

289

But while women such as Benoit Samuelson were woefully undersupported as far as their apparel was concerned, Nike was pushing for gender equity through advocacy. The same year as Benoit's marathon win, "a group of female runners banded together to create the International Runners Committee (IRC) to fight for the inclusion of long-distance running at the Olympic level," states "The Women's Movement," an internal research document that Nike produced in 2012 to review its relationship with the female athlete. In 1979 women were prohibited from running more than 1,500 meters in the Olympics due to a misconception that their bodies were not "built" to withstand long runs. Nike cofounder Phil Knight believed passionately that this should change—and he put Nike money and energy into supporting the IRC.

"The Women's Movement" quotes him:

We were a running shoe company, and we were in the sport. We made shoes for each other. You could go out to an eight-mile road race, which they would have every weekend in Portland, and a third or 40 percent of the contestants were women. So we were just inside the sport enough to know [excluding women's Olympic distance events] was ridiculous. There was no dispute anywhere in the company. We were all pushing for it.

In 1979 Nike released the first in a series of ads supporting the lobby for women's distance events to be added to the Olympics. "We Think It's Time the IOC Stopped Running Away from Women Runners," read the headline, alongside a comic strip-style illustration of a band of strong, lithe women, hair flowing, chasing down three nearly hairless, heavyset older gentlemen. "They say that running a marathon isn't feminine. Women aren't strong enough. Or that not enough countries are interested. Right. . . . We say the members of the IOC have their heads in the sand," Nike's call to action continued below the headline, concluding by asking readers to send letters of support to its world headquarters in Beaverton, Oregon. "We'll collect all the letters in one giant pouch and dump them on the IOC and the IAAF," it promised. Thousands wrote in. "Any time you get that many letters sent to you, it means something," said Rob Strasser, Nike's vice president of marketing at the time.

Nike aligned officially with the IRC soon afterward, and its support paid off. "On February 23, 1981, due to pressure from the IRC and others, the general membership of the International Olympic Committee voted to include the women's 3,000 meters and marathon in the 1984 games," "The Women's Movement" states, "going as far as to ignore a statute that mandated the Olympics wait four years before implementing new sports." Soon after, in 1982, Nike released another ad; this one pictured a fist clenched in victory and read: "The Olympics Will Never Be the Same. They'll be better." This time it called for financial donations to the IRC in order to push for events such as the 5,000 and 10,000 meters to also be included in the Games. The new ad closed: "As marathons go, this one will certainly be the longest. It's taken eighty-eight years just to get to the starting line." When the 1984 games finally took place, Benoit, by then a Nike athlete, won the women's marathon event. She and other women runners like her were finally getting a little of the attention they deserved.

What shorts did they wear to do so? By 1984 the options Nike had available for women were improving, due in no small part to one woman in particular: Diane Katz. Her own story at Nike began in 1978, when Katz was a designer based in Los Angeles but working full-time for Portland-based outerwear company White Stag. "I moved to California, and absolutely everyone was jogging," Katz explained. "And everyone, even when they weren't jogging, [was] wearing waffle trainers." Her boss at the time, John Herman, owned a small apparel company named Sportco, which supplied tricot nylon running shorts to Nike to be silkscreened with the Nike logo—quite likely the same kind of shorts worn by Benoit in 1979. Herman sent a couple of pairs to Katz, the emerging jogger. She was not impressed.

"First of all, they were men's, and second of all, [Sportco] had no one who knew how to design clothing for performance. The whole category hadn't quite been invented yet," Katz reported. "I could barely move, so the next thing was to contact John: 'John, those shorts don't fit. The Nike logo is coming off, and the colors of the shorts don't match the shoes, and you need to tell whoever this guy at Nike is that he needs to, at the very, very least, match the colors to the shoes.'"

FIG 360

WE THINK IT'S TIME THE IOC STOPPED RUNNING AWAY FROM WOMEN RUNNERS.

For some archaic reasons, the International Olympic Committee refuses to allow women runners to compete at any distance longer than 1500 meters.

They say that running a marathon isn't feminine. Women aren't strong enough.

Or that not enough countries are interested. Right. The IOC recognizes things like roque and team epee as Olympic events.

We say the members of the IOC have their heads in the sand.

We'd like to take a stand here for women runners. We've joined the crusade to convince the IOC to allow women to run the distance races just like men do.

And world-class women runners need your help, too. If you agree that women should get equal treatment from the IOC, say so in a letter to us at the address below.

We'll collect all the letters in one giant pouch and dump them on the IOC and the IAAF.

Your letter might make all the difference in getting women in Olympic distance races.

And in getting the IOC off their brains.

World Headquarters
8285 SW Nimbus Avenue, Suite 115
Beaverton, Oregon 97005

Send your letter to the attention of Patsy Mest.

FIG 361

Herman suggested she write to the brand's head of apparel, Roger Knight—which she did, on June 13, 1978 in bright orange ink. "As you may be aware, I am designing both skiwear and sportswear for White Stag, and recently I have also developed a very passionate interest in running!" Katz wrote. "Nike is such a respected name in the running industry that I feel that this identity could be a very marketable commodity in an expanded line of running apparel for both men and (yes, most certainly) WOMEN. In the past few months, I have become painfully aware that the clothing needs of women runners are totally unfulfilled. This is an untapped market of great potential!"

Over the months that followed, Katz secured a retainer with Nike, focusing on athletic apparel. Her time at the brand—in two stints: from 1978 to 1979 and again from 1984 to 1986—was short but extremely impactful. She was the first trained apparel designer the company had ever hired. With her insight, the apparel team and its offering quickly grew.

Now, DNA keeps a binder full of Katz's designs; these early examples are hand-drawn and -colored, with scrawled annotations. She took full advantage of the opportunity to remedy the running shorts that she had so much trouble jogging in in L.A. One sketch from 1978, for the liner or inner brief, shows something of her attention to the all-important details. "Front leg-hole should be cut high and round enough so it sits directly on leg-fold/bend line of body," she wrote. "Back of brief should be cut long and rounded enough to cover well-rounded runner's gluteals. . . . Use lingerie quality elastic around leg to avoid too much constriction." And, crucially, "Develop two patterns—one for men and one for women." In these early suggestions, and others like them, Katz set out the foundations for what Nike's women's shorts would come to be.

Today, no Nike women's shorts are as well-known as the Tempo. They are a phenomenon. They were designed for running and were housed in the running category for many years. But true to the reality of sports clothing—that great design transcends the discipline it was conceived for—they are worn by athletes of all kinds, in all places. Style-wise, they denote an active lifestyle—a sporty type who is planning perhaps to stop by the grocery store before meeting friends for practice later.

The Tempo's status is due, in part, to the fact that they were the shorts that fit women. Their construction was based on a split-leg design created by Nike in the early 1980s, and they could be worn roomy or tight, meaning that they served people whose wide hips, strong thighs, and full glutes were not accommodated in other running shorts. The design had a 3-inch (7.6 cm) inseam rather than the preexisting 1.5-inch (3.8 cm) inseam, providing coverage and a welcome relief from thigh chafe. The Tempo shorts were comfortable, and their price point made them hugely accessible. They were worn for running, tennis, fitness, dance, and other athletics—and because they were worn by women, they became the women's short. In 2024, more than twenty years after they first debuted in 2002, the Tempo remains a best-selling style.

And yet one size, or style, rarely fits all. In track and field as in other arenas, women's uniforms have taken many different forms—from the 1920s, when women's loose, flowing uniforms closely echoed men's, through to the 1980s, when innovations in spandex led to women's uniforms becoming tighter and shorter, until buns, or bundies (briefs, essentially), became the norm. In her book *Coming On Strong: Gender and Sexuality in Women's Sport* (2015), Susan Cahn recognizes the way that women's apparel has been used to temper the masculinity innate in athleticism. Revealing clothing served as proof of femininity. Proof of femininity, through dress, demeanor, and otherwise, became a kind of compensation for sporting excellence.

It's a trend Nike had little to do with enforcing; throughout the 1980s, the company continued to supply its female customer base with the garments they bought and loved: its range of shorts expanded from four styles in 1981 (Relay, Stride, Spirit, and L.A. Sport) to many more by the end of the decade. And yet for the everyday athlete, trends from the world stage slowly trickled down. In recent years, professional athletes have begun pushing back against buns and the like, opting instead to wear loose shorts or bodysuits, revealing or concealing their bodies according to their own preferences. In the process, a pathway has opened up for

THE OFFICIAL DAILY START LISTS & RESULTS

OLYMPIC

DAY 9

PRICE $3.00

RECORD

AUGUST 6 1984

FIG 362

FIG 363

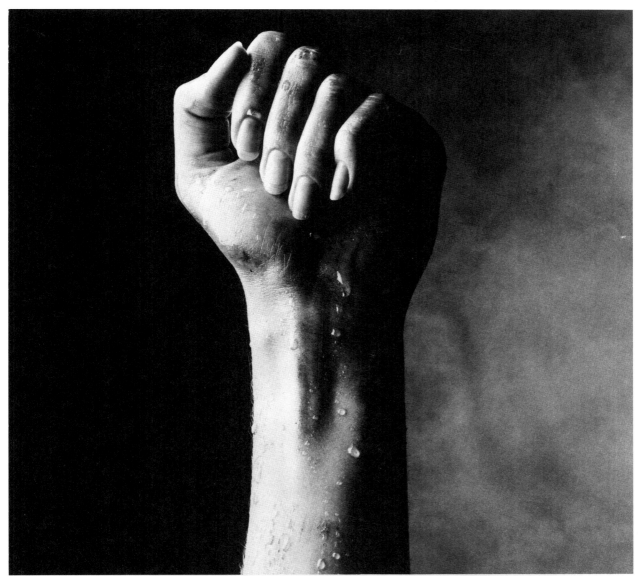

THE OLYMPICS WILL NEVER BE THE SAME.

They'll be better. Because from now on, women will be allowed to run farther than 1,500 meters. Come 1984 and L.A., they will compete in their first Olympic marathon.

It may never have come about if it hadn't been for the International Runners Committee. People like Joe Henderson, Jacqueline Hansen, Nina Kuscsik, Manfred Steffny, Eleanora Mendonca and Dr. Joan Ullyot and many others made the various international bodies recognize women can run. Both fast and far.

For several years, we've chided the IOC and the IAAF for footdragging. And we'd like to take this opportunity to thank them.

But tradition dies hard. While there will be a marathon and a 3,000 meter race for women, there is, as yet, no sanctioned 5,000 meters. Or 10,000 meters.

And odds are there won't be unless the IRC continues to receive financial support. Please help. Send your contributions to IRC, 2011 Kimberly, Eugene, Oregon 97405.

Then come to L.A. and watch the celebration. Because as marathons go, this one will certainly be the longest.

It's taken 88 years just to get to the starting line.

NIKE
Beaverton, Oregon

FIG 364

FIG 365

362 "Olympic Record: The Official Daily Start Lists and Results" program for the 1984 Olympics (detail), 1984

363 "The Olympics Will Never Be the Same" Ad, 1982

364 "We Need More Women Running Washington" featuring Joan Benoit Samuelson (detail), 1989

365 Joan Benoit Samuelson wins the inaugural Olympic Women's Marathon at the Olympic Games in Los Angeles in 1984 (detail)

NIKE OLYMPIC ATHLETE FACT SHEET

JOAN BENOIT

OLYMPIC EVENT:	Marathon	DATE OF BIRTH:	5/16/57
HEIGHT:	1.60 Meters	WEIGHT:	47.17 Kilos
NATIONALITY:	U.S.	BIRTHPLACE:	Portland, Maine
		CLUB/SCHOOL:	Athletics West
MARITAL STATUS:	Single	STUDIES:	Graduate, Boudoin University BA History & Environmental Studies
PROFESSION:	Previously part-time women's coach, Boston University		

CURRENTLY LIVING: Freeport, Maine

BEST TIMES:

```
  4:36       Mile
  9:24       2 Mile
 15:40.47    5K
 32:30       10K
 53:17       10 Mile
1:09:15      1/2 Marathon
1:26:21      25K
2:22:43      Marathon
```


CAREER HIGHLIGHTS:
```
1983       World Record, Marathon
           Time:  2:22:43
1983       American Record, 1/2 Marathon
           Time:  1:09:15
1983       American Record, 10K
           Time:  31:35
1983       Ranked 2nd in the World, Marathon, Track and Field News
1982       American Record, 10 Mile
           Time:  53:17
1981       American Record, 25K
           Time:  1:26:21
```


Note: Information on this fact sheet was collected prior to May 1984.

FIG 366

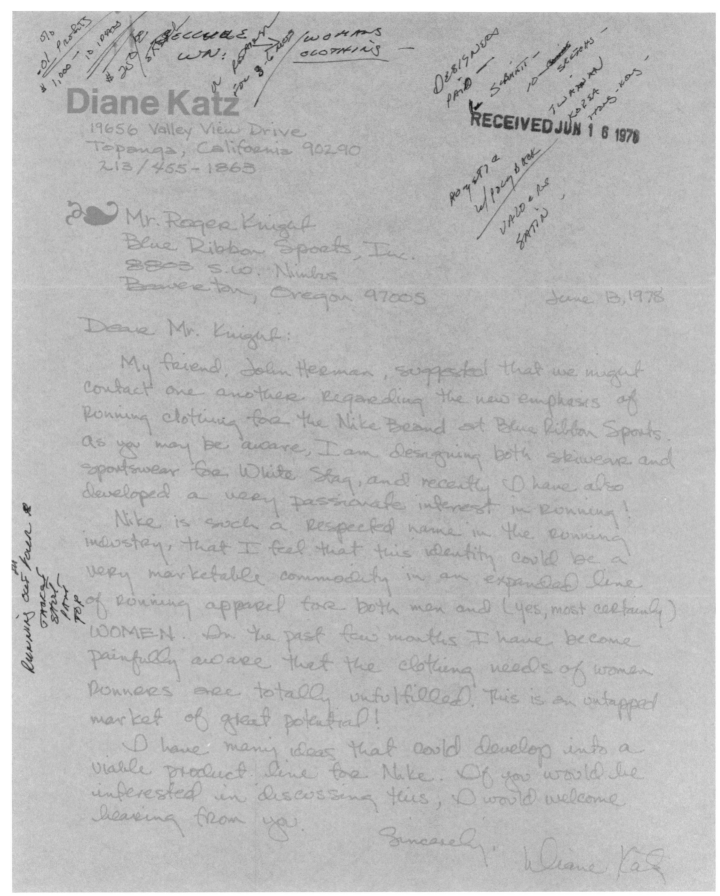

Diane Katz

19656 Valley View Drive
Topanga, California 90290
213/455-1863

RECEIVED JUN 1 6 1978

Mr. Roger Knight
Blue Ribbon Sports, Inc.
8863 S.W. Nimbus
Beaverton, Oregon 97005   June 13, 1978

Dear Mr. Knight:

My friend, John Herman, suggested that we might contact one another regarding the new emphasis of running clothing for the Nike Brand at Blue Ribbon Sports. As you may be aware, I am designing both skiwear and sportswear for White Stag, and recently I have also developed a very passionate interest in running!

Nike is such a respected name in the running industry, that I feel that this identity could be a very marketable commodity in an expanded line of running apparel for both men and (yes, most certainly) WOMEN. In the past few months I have become painfully aware that the clothing needs of women runners are totally unfulfilled. This is an untapped market of great potential!

I have many ideas that could develop into a viable product line for Nike. If you would be interested in discussing this, I would welcome hearing from you.

Sincerely,

Diane Katz

FIG 367

Los Angeles-based designer Diane Katz wrote this letter to former Nike Apparel Director Roger Knight in 1978. Within a year, she became the first ever apparel designer hired by Nike; she joined the brand on a freelance basis to design a line of running clothes on a one-year contract before returning in 1984 to work on the John McEnroe apparel line and the iconic Nike Windrunner Jacket.

366 Joan Benoit Olympic Athlete Fact Sheet, 1984

367 Correspondence between Diane Katz and Roger Knight, 1978

those operating outside of restrictive gender boundaries—including, but not limited to, trans and nonbinary people. For some, loose clothing creates a sense of freedom, both physiologically and socioculturally. In the professional sporting world, a deeply prohibitive and, at times, oppressive space, such victories are important.

On the basketball court, shorts have varied wildly throughout history, veering from long and baggy to short and slim-fitting. Some players roll the waistband to lessen the bulk of fabric or tuck the hem up beneath a spandex underlayer for better freedom and agility. "The NCAA [National Collegiate Athletics Association] men's and women's basketball rule books each devote four and a half pages to uniform regulations, but only one rule—Rule 1, Section 22, Article 10—deals with how players wear them," wrote Daniel Uthman for *USA Today Sports.* "That rule prohibits playing with the jersey untucked from the waistband of the shorts."[1] As for length, that has always been influenced by personal preference, comfort, function, and the style choices of any given era. [On Reddit, some fans argue that it's due to the Hemline Index—a theory positing that skirt (or, in this case, shorts) lengths rise and fall to mirror economic prosperity.[2]]

In a pickup game, you'll see basketball players pushing their style choices to the limits—wearing elaborate layers, volumes, shapes, jewelry. It's often the governing bodies, then, who make the rules about what can be worn and when. When those rules accommodate personal preference and individuality, the whole sport wins. More recently the WNBA has expanded its uniform offering to include shorts of three lengths: knee-length, above knee-length, and below knee-length, allowing players to choose their uniform according to their preferences. This move marked a revolution in the way the sporting world thinks about team uniforms and gives a nod to the fact that every player need not, let alone cannot, look the same. Such options are "extremely important," says WNBA standout Sabrina Ionescu. "It allows you to be who you want to be."[3]

For people who menstruate, shorts have another part to play: they're the final frontier against bleed-through. Young women between the ages of ten and twelve are the most likely to stop participating in sports, and periods are at least partly responsible. In 2023 Nike released Leak Protection: Period, a new innovation in which an ultrathin, absorbent liner was incorporated into the Nike One shorts for women and girls to help protect against leakage of all kinds. The designers behind the project used significant materials validation and wear-testing, with the aim of delivering a pair of shorts that could be paired with the wearer's preferred

368

FIG 368

FIG 369

368 Swoosh Shorts design sketches by Diane Katz (details), 1978

369 Diane Katz working on apparel designs at her home office in Mill Valley, California, 1979

370 Running Shorts design by Diane Katz, 1978

371 Swoosh Shorts design sketch by Diane Katz (detail), 1978

period product—whether a tampon, pad, or cup. A two-layer laminate gusset in the invisible built-in brief absorbs, wicks, and holds blood and other fluids, while a membrane acts as a barrier against leakage. The team worked through thirty prototypes to find the best fit for movement and comfort to suit wearers from adolescence through to advanced age. For elite athletes, the technology debuted on the football field in the Nike Pro Short, the base layer offered to players at the 2023 Women's World Cup.

In connected developments, that same World Cup saw fewer white shorts as part of national uniforms than any previous year. England, New Zealand, Canada, France, and Nigeria—countries that had worn white shorts four years earlier—all moved toward other, more forgiving colors. The US team opted out of white shorts for the first time since the Women's World Cup was formalized in 1991.[4]

On the court, the battle has stretched on even longer. Tennis is a sport rooted in antiquated ideas about what women should and shouldn't wear. In the 1920s French player Suzanne Lenglen was beloved for her grace and style, which contributed to the era's celebration of female athleticism. For the first time in modern history, women were encouraged in sporting pursuits—not least because the exercise would help them to achieve and maintain the slim physique that the era's flapper fashions demanded, with their focus on straight lines and "boyish" cuts. But Lenglen also shocked audiences, wearing gauzy, lightweight tennis dresses that exposed her muscular body and bare, tanned arms.[5] She embodied strength, freedom, power, and agility, and she did it all on the court, in style.

By the 1940s and 1950s, some tennis players had begun wearing shorts to increase their mobility, and for modesty, beneath the short dresses and skirts that were becoming the fashion. But ideas about what was "proper" were slippery: in 1949 Gertrude "Gussie" Moran competed at Wimbledon wearing a pair of lace-trimmed shorts beneath her dress, an outfit designed by designer Teddy Tinling. "The All England Club's committee was horrified, and criticized her for bringing 'vulgarity and sin into tennis,'" wrote Paul Newman in the *Independent*. "The subject was even raised in parliament."[6]

As the years have passed, the rules around wearing shorts alone in the Grand Slams have remained somewhat ambiguous; while governing bodies don't explicitly ban female players from competing in them without an additional layer on top, expectation has often overruled the stated codes. So while many players practice in shorts, most will usually wear a skirt or dress to compete. These additional layers can put players

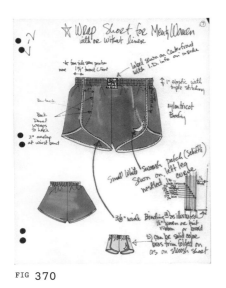

FIG 370

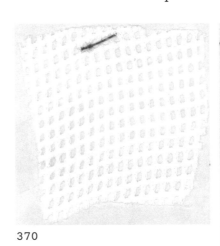

370

FIG 371

370

368

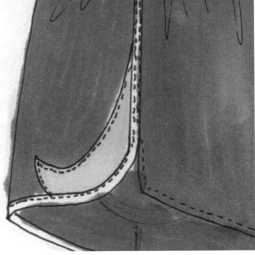

368

#1004

(2)

Two-Color Jacquard Knit insert.
Jacquard must be done in Nylon,
But try to get Acrylic or cotton/poly

CHAIN swoosh
Short

White
Black
Black
White
Black
White
Black

total width
jacquard 1⅛"

⊛ Back same as
front

side view

¼"
contrast
nylon tricot
folded over
edge & flatted on
jacquard insert

Bar tack

Bar tack
Black &
White Jacquard

* Navy Tricot
- Navy Orange Chain
- White Bias Trim

1-18-79

FIG 372

298

FIG 373

FIG 374

FIG 375

372 Chain Swoosh on Short design by Diane Katz, 1979

373 Nylon Tricot Sport Co. Shorts with Nike Logo, 1975

374 Gazelle Shorts, 1983

375 Relay Shorts (detail), 1991

at a thermoregulatory disadvantage, inhibit movement, and slow them down. Male athletes, of course, are not held to the same arbitrary and outdated ideas.

The color white remains pervasive throughout tennis—particularly, and most famously, at Wimbledon. The tournament's all-white dress code was first implemented to camouflage sweat stains but was retained by Wimbledon to help set it apart from the likes of the French, Australian, and US Opens.[7] These outdated rules meant female players were forbidden from wearing shorts in any color other than white. During menstruation, leakage was, therefore, a very real fear. Former world number one Billie Jean King has been instrumental in changing that. King, who won thirty-nine Grand Slam titles over the course of her career, as well as the famous Battle of the Sexes against Bobby Riggs in 1973, has become one of the sport's most vocal advocates for social justice and gender equality. "My generation, we always worried because we wore all white all the time," King told CNN's Amanda Davies. "And it's what you wear underneath that's important for your menstrual period. And we're always checking whether we're showing. You get tense about it because the first thing we are is entertainers, and you want whatever you wear to look immaculate, look great."[8] In 2023, in a landmark and long-overdue shift, the All England Lawn Tennis and Croquet Club at last relaxed its rules in recognition of the issues menstruating athletes faced at Wimbledon, and competitors were permitted to wear dark shorts under their tennis whites.[9] For onlookers around the world, it sparked a new question: why did it take so long?

Hemlines, color palettes, inseam lengths. These are details that can make or break women's sporting experiences, their performances, and even their capacity to play in the first place. Their stories are powerful, political, and important; they make tangible the proverbial blood, sweat, and tears and demand better for their successors. In a world defined by rules of play, sports' governing bodies dismiss their calls for change at their own risk. Women are on the field, and they're determined to level it.

— 1 —

Daniel Uthman, "For College Basketball Players, Long Shorts Might Finally Be Taking a Seat," *USA Today Sports*, March 08, 2017, eu.usatoday.com/story/sports/ncaab/2017/03/08/college-basketball-short-shorts-michael-jordan-fab-five/98891284.

— 2 —

"What's the Deal with NBA Shorts? Who Decides When and What's Considered Before the Shorts Change?," NBA community forum, Reddit, 2022, www.reddit.com/r/nba/comments/x5dfeh/whats_the_deal_with_nba_shorts_who_decides_when.

— 3 —

Sabrina Ionescu, interviewed by Vanessa Friedman, "From the Women's World Cup to Wimbledon, a Victory Everyone Can Share," *New York Times*, August 8, 2023, www.nytimes.com/2023/08/08/style/womens-sports-uniforms-change.

— 4 —

Friedman, "From the Women's World Cup." 2023.

— 5 —

Susan Cahn, *Coming on Strong: Gender and Sexuality in Women's Sport* (Boston: Harvard University Press, 1995).

— 6 —

Paul Newman, "Gussie Moran: Tennis Player Who Shocked Wimbledon With Her Controversial Clothing," *Independent*, January 20, 2013, www.independent.co.uk/news/obituaries/gussie-moran-tennis-player-who-shocked-wimbledon-with-her-controversial-clothing-8459119.

— 7 —

Issy Ronald and Amanda Davies, "Wimbledon in Discussions About Changing Its All-White Uniform Policy After Billie Jean King Reveals It Is Her 'Pet Peeve,'" *CNN*, November 8, 2022, www.edition.cnn.com/2022/11/07/tennis/billie-jean-king-jacket-periods-wimbledon-spt-intl/index.

— 8 —

Ronald and Davies, "Wimbledon in Discussions," 2022.

— 9 —

Friedman, "From the Women's World Cup," 2023.

FIG 376

FIG 377

Spring '83 Sports Apparel

FIG 378

NIKE COMES UP SHORT.

When it's time to let your legs do the talking, let them speak freely. In Nike running shorts. We've got the models for every build, for every running style. From the conventional, to high European leg cut, to the split-leg. In styles for men. Styles for women. We also have the most revolutionary shorts on the market—Nike Running Lites. They're made from one ounce nylon Ripstop— a material so light it's used for making kites. So whether you're on the line for the year's most important race, or just another training run, slip into Nike. And make short work of it.

NIKE

Beaverton, Oregon

FIG 379

376 Cover of Nike Apparel Catalogue (detail), 1981

377 Sports Apparel Catalog, Spring 1983

378 Running Lites in "Nike Comes Up Short, 1982

379 Nike Rival Shorts (detail), 1985

FIG 380

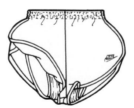

FIG 381

FIG 382

380 "For Women Only" poster, 1988

381 Split Leg Short, Spring 1989

382 Elite Racer Shorts, 1985

383 International Singlet and International Ripstop Short, Spring 1991

384 "Just Do It 365" featuring Lynn Jennings, 1990

385 Color Pallette, Spring 1991

386 Supplex Short, Spring 1989

FIG 383

FIG 384

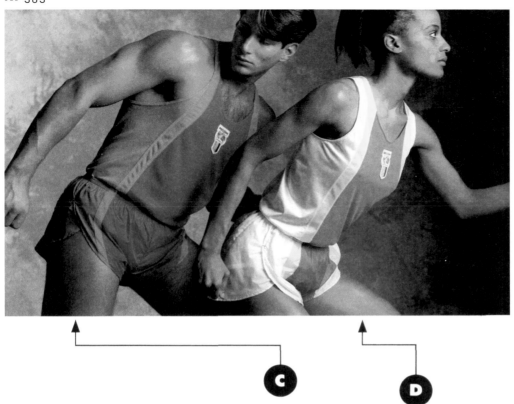

C

D

just do it³⁶⁵

384

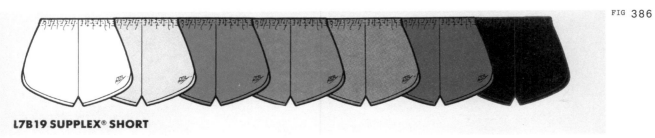

FIG 385

FIG 386

L7B19 SUPPLEX® SHORT

303

FIG 387

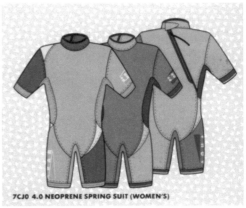

7CJ0 4.0 NEOPRENE SPRING SUIT (WOMEN'S)

FIG 388

FIG 389

AQUA GEAR

1CE0 SONORA BAY NYLON/ LYCRA® SHORT (UNISEX)

SuperSlick 82% nylon/18% Lycra® tricot, narrow cut mid-thigh length short with contoured elastic waist, outside drawcord with rubber Lace-Lock™ exit system, side panel insets, inside right front key pocket, embossed rubber AQUA GEAR trademark patch at lower left leg
12/25 Delivery

02	Bright Pink/Chlorine Blue/Sunbeam				20.00	40.00
21	Scream Green/Eggplant/Vivid Grape					
42	Eggplant/Amethyst/Bright Pink					
58	Black/Chlorine Blue/Amethyst					

▼

In 1990, Nike released Aqua Gear, its first collection for surfing, windsurfing, and sailing. The range included reversible nylon jackets and bright volleyball shorts, designated by the *Los Angeles Times* as appropriate for the "casual beachcomber," and performance vests and shorts created to protect in water temperatures as low as 60 degrees Fahrenheit.

387 Page from Women's Apparel Catalog, Spring 1991

388 Neoprene Spring Suit (Women's), Spring 1991

389 International Singlet, 1993

390 International Singlet and International Short, Spring 1992

391 Fitness Short, Spring 1993

392 Fitness Short, Spring 1994

393 Hood River IV Short, Spring 1992

FIG 390

FIG 391

220194 FITNESS SHORT		$15.00/$30.00
050	Grey Heather	
010	Black	
100	White	

FIG 392

202003-527
202003-010

FIG 393

FIG 394

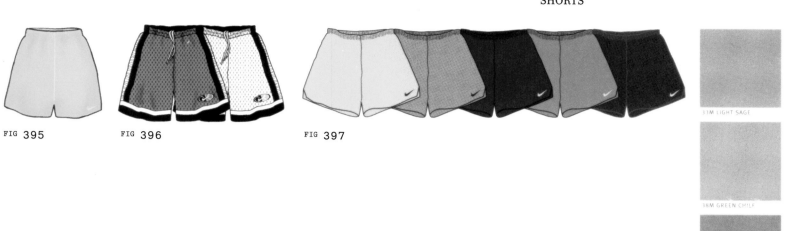

FIG 395   FIG 396   FIG 397

33M LIGHT SAGE

38M GREEN CHILE

31T PEAR

16X PALM GREEN

FIG 398

  FALL 1998

FIG 399

398

01E NEUTRAL GREY

10A WHITE

FIG 400

401

FIG 402

ultra short-sleeve top
ultra tank

premiere split-leg short

400

SUMMER 2008_APPAREL

WOMEN'S

FIG 403

308

400 Cover of Women's Apparel Catalog (detail), Summer 2008

401 Tempo Track Shorts, 2007

402 Ultra Short-Sleeve Top, Ultra Tank, and Premiere Split-Leg Short, Summer 2005

403 Flex Dri-FIT Tank and Short in "Sends Sweat To The Locker Room" featuring Tisha Venturini (detail), 2000

404 Tempo Track Short, Holiday 2003

405 Tempo Short

FIG 404

FIG 405

405

FIG 406

FIG 407

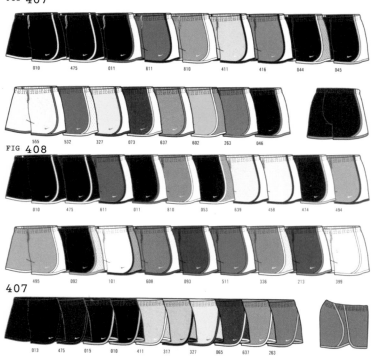

010 475 011 611 810 411 416 044 045

555 532 327 073 637 602 263 046

FIG 408

010 475 611 011 810 053 639 458 474 494

495 092 101 608 093 511 336 213 399

407

013 475 015 010 411 317 327 065 637 263

FIG 409

406 Rocky Shorts, 1991

407 Tempo Track Short and Sister Tempo Short, Summer 2008

408 Tempo Track Short, Fall 2009

409 Tempo Printed Modern Short, Fall 2014

410 Modern Embossed Tempo Shorts, 2015

411 Tempo Short, Summer 2013

412 Fast Tempo Running Shorts

FIG 410

967   972

FIG 411

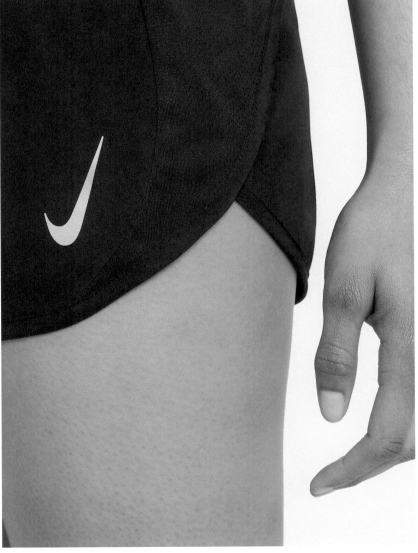

FIG 412

FIG 413

The Nike Air Transition, available in nine team colors.

FIG 414

FIG 415

FIG 416

FIG 417

220650 DURASHEEN MESH BASKETBALL SHORT

CONTENT: 100% polyester.
PROFILE: Durasheen front and back, double-layer side mesh panels, inside drawcord, striped rib-knit waistband and cuffs, embroidered Swoosh design trademark at lower left front of leg.
WHOLESALE: $19.00   **SUGGESTED RETAIL:** $38.00

417

413 Air Transition in "If You've Got A Problem, Get Over It," 1990

414 Arella Guirantes during the FIBA Women's Basketball World Cup, 2022

415 Women's Apparel Catalog (detail), Fall 2004'

416 Durasheen Mesh Basketball Short, Fall 1996

417 Women's Apparel Catalog (detail), Fall 1996

011 012 013 057 065 066

342 420 451 453 494 496

546 612 658 670 676 678

784 821

FIG 418

418 Women's Up and Under Short, Fall 2012

419 Hoops Durasheen Short, Fall 2004

420 Page from Women's Apparel Catalog, Spring 1997

421 Knit Basketball Short, Holiday 2013

422 Tongton Wu during the FIBA Women's Basketball World Cup, 2022

423 Sabrina Ionescu during a WNBA game, 2023

FIG 419

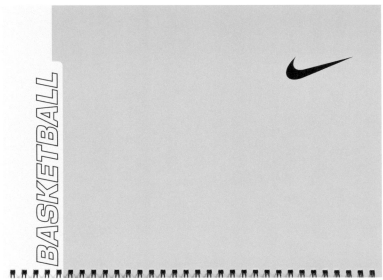

BASKETBALL

FIG 420

FIG 421

FIG 422

423

Following page:

FIG 424   FIG 425

DRESS TO KILL.

Once that little door closes behind you, there's no such thing as mercy.

You're going to be jammed. Jarred. Driven into the wall. By some of the nicest people you know. About the time you're totally stressed-out, they'll rip a 100 mph shot into the corner.

Take a tip from the pros. The first chance you get, move in for the kill. Move into Nike.

We've got the shoes that know how to hold center court. For any level of play.

Take our Killshots in the photo. Their bi-level hobnail cupsole gives you traction for the most sudden move. In any direction. And the open toe design lets you accomplish it in total comfort. Naturally, there are both men's and women's models, with mesh uppers so they

breathe, and suede toe caps so they last.

We can even give you some help upstairs. With court attire made for the most grueling match. Lightweight. Durable. Designed and cut so you never feel hemmed in.

Obviously, when you come dressed in Nike, you'll look terrific.

But in this outfit, looks can kill.

NIKE Beaverton, Oregon

FIG 426

FIG 427

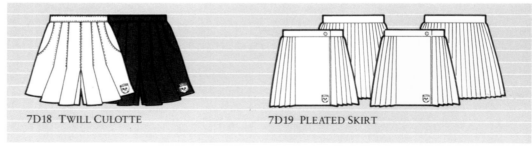

7D18 TWILL CULOTTE   7D19 PLEATED SKIRT

428 Jersey Tank and Pique Print Short, Spring 1987

429 Cover of Women's Apparel Catalog, Spring 1990

430 Page from Women's Apparel Catalog, Fall 1988

431 Tennis Apparel Pattern by Amanda Briggs

FIG 428

FIG 429

FIG 430

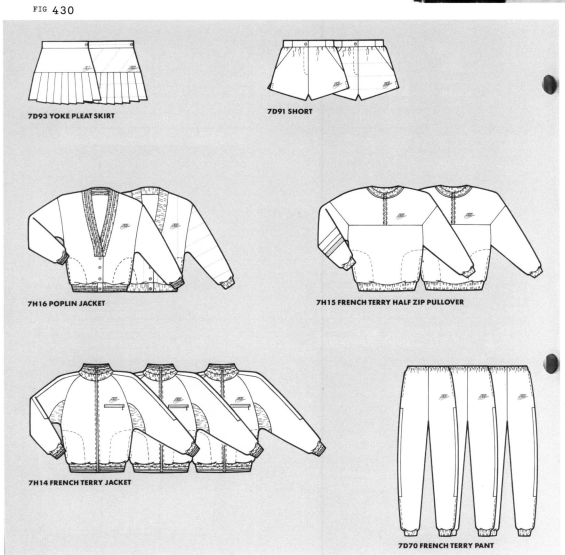

7D93 YOKE PLEAT SKIRT

7D91 SHORT

7H16 POPLIN JACKET

7H15 FRENCH TERRY HALF ZIP PULLOVER

7H14 FRENCH TERRY JACKET

7D70 FRENCH TERRY PANT

FIG 431

FIG 432

FIG 433

FIG 434

FIG 435

240340 · 100
240199 · 100

240339 · 010
240199 · 425

you want to play
so play

you want to **be strong**
so be strong
you want this world to know you are alive
so be alive
play everything as if you
could not **live without it**

JUST DO IT

FIG 436

FIG 437

432 Denim Shorts, 1991

433 Jersey Short, Spring 1994

434 "What's To Lose?" featuring Mary Pierce, 1997

435 Short-Sleeve V-Neck Tee, Court Skirt, and Dri-FIT Short-Sleeve Top, Holiday 1997

436 "You Want to Play So Play," 1994

437 Cover of Men's, Women's & Kids' Apparel Catalog (detail), Summer 1997

FIG 438

320

FIG 439

FIG 440

FIG 441

FIG 442

438 Apparel Inspiration Sketches by Serena Williams, 2006

439 Cover of Women's Apparel Catalog (detail), Fall 1996

440 Dri-FIT Pocketed Bloomer, Holiday 1997

441 2007 Wimbledon Tennis Shorts made for Serena Williams, 2007

442 1999 Wimbledon Dri-FIT ID Tennis Skirt worn by Lindsay Davenport

FIG 443

FIG 444

FIG 445

This dress, which was created for Serena Williams to wear at Wimbledon in 2019, features cutouts at the sides and a gold and diamante Swoosh pinned at the front left chest. Wimbledon 2019 marked the 13th year in a row that Williams played. She lost in the final match to Simona Halep, a fellow Nike tennis athlete.

443 2019 Wimbledon NikeCourt Dress made for Serena Williams, 2019

444 2008 Wimbledon Dress made for Serena Williams, 2008

445 Serena Williams at the Wimbledon Lawn Tennis Championships, London, 2015

445

FIG 446

FIG 447

FIG 448

448

In spring 2023, Nike released Leak Protection: Period, an ultra-thin, absorbent liner incorporated first within the Nike One Short silhouette to help protect against leaks. The short has a supportive 7-inch inseam and invisible built-in brief, providing comfort and confidence to people who menstruate.

446 US National Team 1996 Atlanta Olympics Shorts autographed by Mia Hamm, 1996

447 US Women's National Team Shorts, 2016

448 Nike One Leak Protection: Period Mid-rise Biker Shorts

FIG 449

448

FIG 451

FIG 452

FIG 450

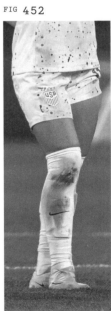

449 Abby Wambach plays for the USWNT, 2015

450 Nike Pro Leak Protection Period Girls Dri-FIT Leggings (detail)

451 Nigeria Shorts, 2023

452 USWNT Shorts, 2023

September 10, 2016. Rio de Janeiro, Brazil.

Scout Bassett flies through the air in the women's long jump T42 final at the Rio 2016 Paralympic Games.

May 8, 2022. Las Vegas, USA.

A'ja Wilson of the Las Vegas Aces drives against Sue Bird of the Seattle Storm.

September 9, 2008. Beijing, China.

Tatyana McFadden races in the women's 100-meter T54 at the 2008 Paralympic Games.

ATHLETE: SCOUT BASSETT

SUBJECT: MODIFYING HER TIGHTS

BIOGRAPHY: Scout Bassett is an American track-and-field athlete who competes in the
100-, 200-, 400-meter sprints, and the long jump, in the T42 classification.
She was born in 1988 in Nanjing, China.

I'm an above-knee amputee, and I have different legs to switch out—

my running leg and my walking leg.

I love the look of tights, but the only way I could wear them and change my leg was by completely taking them off.

When you're at an outdoor track or a training venue, there's not always an appropriate place to do that,

so I didn't wear tights for a long time.

One day, I decided to cut them;

I made [one side] short enough that it would fit like shorts on the side with the prosthetic, so that I could switch out my legs seamlessly.

It didn't have to be this whole scene; I didn't have to go to the bathroom or drop my pants in public.

I started altering that leg in all my tights.

It was very functional;

I took something that wasn't accessible to amputees, I modified it, and I love wearing tights as a result.

I take a lot of pride in it, because so many people who have disabilities, particularly amputees, have told me,

'I started doing this because I saw you do it.'

ATHLETE: SUE BIRD

SUBJECT: SHORTS

BIOGRAPHY: Sue Bird is an American basketball player. She was
born in 1980 in New York, USA.

One of my biggest complaints throughout my time as an athlete was that the clothes were always so big.

There was a period of time when you always had to wear mens'.

I don't have the same body type as a guy, so a lot of the shorts were long and narrow, and I literally could never wear them.

They're not built for anybody who has any kind of hip whatsoever.

Nowadays, it's different. It's not one-size-fits-all.

They started adding length to the uniform.

So yes, my teammates who loved long shorts could get the plus-two, plus-four length, and then someone like me could just get the regulars,

and they would actually fit.

It is definitely an expression.

Look at A'ja Wilson. She likes to wear her shorts short; she tucks them in a lot.

Diana Taurasi would never be caught dead in anything where you can see her knees, basically; she loves her shorts super, super long.

Everybody has their preference, their style,

and now you're seeing people stand up for themselves with that,

whereas even ten years ago, you sucked it up and wore it, because you didn't really have that voice.

That's definitely changing.

ATHLETE: TATYANA MCFADDEN

SUBJECT: GLOVES

BIOGRAPHY: Tatyana McFadden is an American track-and-field athlete who competes in the
100-, 200-, 400-, 4×100-, 800-, 1500-, and 5000-meter races in the T54 classification, and the marathon. She was born in 1989 in Saint Petersburg, Russia.

Innovation and technology are really important in our sport,

and gloves are important in all weather.

When I started competing, I was first in harness gloves that fit like a mitten, with straps.

By the time I got to Beijing, we'd transitioned into making hard gloves out of plastic Aquaglass beads.

I'd get out my mom's worst frying pan,

dump the plastic beads in boiling water, then take it out with tongs while it [was] hot and very melted and mold it in my hands.

You had to treat them like they were your child;

they couldn't be sat out in the sun, or in extreme cold weather, because they'd melt or crack.

For the longest time I was carrying a racing glove on my lap everywhere I went at competition, so they wouldn't get destroyed before a race.

Eventually they would thin right down because of the pounding on the chair and the heat in your hands.

The gloves that I wear to compete now are 3D-printed, a mix of plastic and carbon.

Now you can find a style you really like and 3D-print it.

Anything can happen to them, and it's okay;

you just hit *print*.

ATHLETE: **KIRSTY GODSO**

SUBJECT: TAKING YOURSELF SERIOUSLY

BIOGRAPHY: Kirsty Godso is a Nike master trainer. She was born
in 1988 in Auckland, New Zealand.

When you put on Nike, it makes you feel like you're taking yourself seriously.

It's not designed for 'you're gonna look cute, and your boobs are gonna be pushed up'. No.

It's about, 'I am here for you in your body;

let's do this together'.

adapt

and

evolve

natalie e. wright

Speed is a fundamental metric for athletic performance. Clothing designers spend years in research, development, and testing to make minute modifications—an adjusted seam, an updated textile—that might allow an individual athlete to shave hundredths, or even thousandths of a second from their recorded time. The urge for improvement pushes many places beyond the decimal point, usually with the medal stand in mind. Designers' careers are built off the back of it.

For disabled people, an awareness of speed is woven throughout the fabric of day-to-day life. Many of our current beliefs about time and speed date back to the turn of the twentieth century, and inventions such as the automobile, the zipper, the escalator, and the "moving pavement," an antecedent to today's moving walkways.[1] Just as the world felt as though it was speeding up, intellectual disability became synonymous with "slowness."[2] Diagnostic terms such as "delayed" came into common usage, compounding the connection. Slow, society inadvertently declared, equaled bad. Today, disabled athletes are some of the most visible disabled people in society challenging this notion. Less visible is the adaptation and evolution of clothing design.

Where important progress has been made in clothing design for disability since the mid-twentieth century, it has largely focused on everyday wear, not sports apparel. Athletes with disabilities make do with obstructive garments, or tailor garments to their needs, evolving their form or technique to work around the limitations of the equipment available. Upon reaching a certain level, they rely on partnerships with brands or educational institutions for high-end performance wear.[3] These adaptations can foreground monumental shifts.

Take, for instance, American track-and-field Paralympian Scout Bassett, who has been a powerful campaigner for more accessible activewear. Bassett lost her right leg and left big toe in a chemical fire as a baby in China, and at seven years old she moved to the United States with her adoptive family. From the early stages of her career, running shoes posed a problem. The smallest women's track spikes she could find were still too big; she stuffed them with socks to make them usable. Upon signing with Nike in 2015, Bassett received her first pair of custom-made spikes. They were designed to provide stability without flexing too much in motion and to minimize the time the foot spent on the ground when it made contact. She immediately reduced her 100-meter time from 19 to 17 seconds. "To drop more than two seconds in 100 meters is just crazy," she told *Women's Health*. "And it goes to show what a difference adaptive activewear can make."[4] On the track, Bassett describes the power of altering the length of one leg of her running leggings, allowing her to switch her prosthetics without the need to undress altogether—a slow and inconvenient process, particularly if a changing room is not close at hand.

Away from sporting spaces, an individual's mastery of the elements that go into getting dressed—such as pulling on pants, buttoning buttons,

1

Enda Duffy, *The Speed Handbook: Velocity, Pleasure, Modernism* (Durham: Duke University Press, 2009), 4.

2

See, for example, D.P. MacMillan, "The Examination of Exceptional Children," *Pediatrics* 21, no. 5 (May, 1909): 276.

3

For an example of a partnership with an educational institution, see, Rosemary Feitelberg, "Parsons and Special Olympics Working to Create Sustainable Change in Inclusive Apparel," *Women's Wear Daily*, May 7, 2021, www.com/fashion-news/fashion-features/parsons-special-olympics-nigel-barker-inclusive-design-adaptive-apparel-1234819093.

4

Scout Bassett and Alexis Jones, "Paralympian Scout Bassett: Women With Disabilities Are Seen As Weak. The Right Activewear Can Help Change That," *Women's Health*, October 9, 2020, www.womenshealthmag.com/fitness/a32998687/scout-bassett-adaptive-clothing.

tying shoes—has been one timescale used to measure their "developmental progress." How long is an "appropriate" amount of time to get dressed? The mundane nature of dressing belies its complexity; it requires balance, strength, dexterity, and flexibility, as well as an understanding of how to sequence each garment. In the 1977 publication *Dressing for Disabled People*, the number one requirement for dressing is stated as "The need for time."[5] The authors lamented that caregivers too often enforced rigid and arbitrary timelines for dressing, only to then inevitably dress the individual themselves when he or she "failed." In the twentieth century, the stakes were high: one's ability to dress oneself could mean the difference between institutionalization, or not. Today, disabled folks discuss the experience of "crip time," a more flexible approach to time that liberates disabled persons from disciplinary time.[6] Tasks may take longer. Other things may happen quickly—aging, for example, or Bassett's 100-meter dash.

Sport, of course, is not limited to sporting spaces. It can be extrapolated to athleticism or physicality—and a person's ease of movement in their garments is one way to access these ideas. Designers working on clothing for disability in the mid-twentieth century, for instance, had to account for the muscular builds that disabled women developed from operating mobility aids like wheelchairs and crutches.[7] These individuals' body shapes changed as their arms and shoulders grew larger, demanding different shapes from their apparel. At the same time, these designers learned that disabled women perspired more while undertaking daily tasks—including dressing and undressing—because of the added difficulty that their impairments caused.[8]

Sports, disability, clothing, and speed, then, are intimately connected. Today, custom-made and bespoke solutions provide a gold standard—but they are often far from accessible for the amateur disabled sportsperson. Nonetheless, the changes in attitudes and ideas that prepared the way for the likes of Scout Bassett's running shoes are rooted in historical shifts and disabled expertise. Experimentation, modification, and transformation were born out of ideas that now feel ordinary, such as small buttons are fiddly and impractical—can we create a faster way to attach a skirt? Could a pleat give the wearer more room to move their arms in this jacket? What if we could invent a fabric with so much stretch that we do away with the need for fastenings altogether?

By reading between the lines of documents, newspaper articles, photographs, and illustrations from before 1979, when Nike's apparel division was created, a history of women, sports, and disability emerges. It is concentrated in the developments that have dripped slowly into the cultural consciousness—from fastenings and fabrics to fits.

Here, I'll explore a handful of these historical adaptations that have precipitated extraordinary improvements for disabled athletes—garments slipped effortlessly on; seconds shaved off. In looking back over the archive, the sketches, and the patterns, we examine what has come before. And from them, we ask—what's next?

The mundane nature of dressing belies its complexity; it requires balance,

strength,

dexterity,

and flexibility.

— 5 —

Rosemary Ruston, *Dressing for Disabled People* (London: The Disabled Living Foundation, 1977), 15.

— 6 —

Alison Kafer, "Time for Disability Studies and a Future for Crips," in *Feminist, Queer, Crip* (Bloomington: Indiana University Press, 2013), 25–46; Ellen Samuels, "Six Ways of Looking at Crip Time," *Disability Studies Quarterly* 37, no. 3 (Summer 2017): www.dsq-sds.org/index.php/dsq/article/view/5824/4684.

— 7 —

Helen Cookman and Muriel Zimmerman, *Functional Fashions for the Physically Handicapped* (New York: Institute for Physical Medicine and Rehabilitation, 1961), 11.

— 8 —

Clarice L. Scott, "Clothes for the Physically Handicapped Homemaker," United States Department of Agriculture, 12 (June, 1961): 4.

ZIPPERS

"Zip" means fast—synonyms include "energy," "get-up-and-go," "dynamism," and "vigor"—but zippers were made and sold for almost thirty years before they took on this name. Whitcomb Judson patented the first "slide fastener" in 1893, which he designed as a clasp for shoes; initially, the zipper opened and closed two strands of alternating hooks and eyes, leading to the company's name Automatic Hook and Eye. One of the first prototypes, named the C-curity Fastener, was used in women's skirts. But there were major problems—it came apart when the user bent over, for one.[9]

It wasn't until 1917 that Swedish-American engineer Gideon Sundback created the "hookless" fastener, which used interlocking "scoops" to solve the problem. Some of the first uses for the hookless fastener were in sports clothing, such as a women's riding skirt with zippers at the front and back to open when the rider mounted, and to close when she dismounted.[10] In the following years, Sundback continued to create variations on the design, including one he called "the one-handed slider"—an invocation of both disability and efficiency.[11] It was in the 1920s that the zipper got its name when Goodrich created galoshes with the fastener, and the company's president enthusiastically called them "Zippers." Meanwhile, another company was securing the Canadian market under the name "Lightning Fastener Company."[12] Speed, indeed.

Zippers had a key part to play in bringing about the twentieth century's focus on the importance of dressing oneself. One 1930 ad for Talon, Inc. zippers, read, "1 . . . 2 . . . 3 and she's dressed herself. [. . .] The self-dress idea: a new convenience in children's clothing. . . welcomed by children and mothers alike. [. . .] Talon-fastened clothes teach self-reliance and sturdy independence to the youngsters in a practical way they'll like."[13]

This emphasis on independence was novel; while individuals have dressed themselves throughout history, for centuries, it was aspirational to have aid. The complex layered garments that upper-class women wore in the Renaissance through to the Victorian era, for example, were made for staff, or even enslaved persons, to dress the wearer in. It is possible that we experience vestiges of this history in our everyday clothing today—in, for example, the left-facing buttons on women's garments, which are so placed to face the person(s) doing the dressing, rather than the wearer.[14]

In the twentieth century, there became an expectation with moral valence that individuals should dress themselves. A combination of factors influenced this change, including where and how caregiving took place. At the time of Talon, Inc.'s advertisement, for example, the government established federally funded nursery schools. Home economists lobbied for children's garments that promoted self-dressing to ease the responsibilities of those in charge of caring for many children at one time.[15]

The ease and speed that zippers promised increased pressure for disabled persons to dress autonomously. Yet they also made certain accessible features possible—such as trouser-leg openings—to help the wearer reach this goal.[16] It wasn't until later in the twentieth century that disability advocates fought to change the cultural paradigm from independence to interdependence to normalize aid.

ACTION PLEATS

In the late 1950s and early 1960s, designers of clothing for disability began using "action pleats" to extend the wearer's movement. These were, in effect, box pleats that opened when the user reached up or forward. Today, the term "action pleat" or "action back" is most closely associated with men's Norfolk Jackets; these English tweed jackets feature box pleats at the front and back, and are thought to have come about in the 1860s for sporting activities such as hunting, in which context they enabled men to raise their arms comfortably to shoot.[17]

It was around the 1930s, however, that the term "action" came into play to describe this technical application—particularly for women. Reporting on a 1926 fashion show at J. A. Rudy & Son's department store, one reporter wrote, "If there is any one thing expressed more than another in Rudy's frocks and coats, it is ACTION. Pleats and fullness in skirts, pleats and capes on coats, emphasize this youthful quality."[18]

Two years later, "action pleats" were a value-added quality that advertisers emphasized for women's garments, both for everyday and sports such as tennis and golf.[19] By 1936, *Vogue* reported on "Three New Outfits for Tennis and Three New Outfits for Golf Together with Helpful Suggestions to Make the Best of Your Game." Asking for the latter, "Is the blouse equipped with an action pleat or fullness in back?"[20] It wasn't activewear, the magazine suggested, unless it featured action pleats.

Accessible clothing designers in the mid-twentieth century were reprising this feature when they used it for disability. Clothing specialist Clarice L. Scott discussed action pleats in her 1959 article "Clothing Needs of Physically Handicapped Homemakers." Scott worked for the United States Government's Department of Agriculture, and interviewed seventy physically disabled women in her home of Washington, DC. One of the problem garments for women was blouses. "When a woman must work from her chair," Scott learned, "her clothes are strained by long reaches up, forward, and down."[21] This caused blouse backs to split, armholes to tear, and waistlines to rip. In her section "Action Features," Scott reported that her sample of women had unwittingly favored garments in their wardrobes with action pleats without necessarily knowing to seek these out while shopping.[22] In her 1961 clothing line, each top included at least one "action feature" in the form of back pleats, underarm extensions, or even hidden waistline pleats.

While Scott's line wasn't available in stores, pattern companies developed some of her designs for women to make at home. One newspaper article

9   Robert Friedel, *Zipper: An Exploration in Novelty* (New York: W. W. Norton, 1994), 41–2, 50.

10   Friedel, *Zipper*, 129.

11   Friedel, *Zipper*, 135–6.

12   Friedel, *Zipper*, 156.

13   Friedel, *Zipper*, 178.

14   Caitlin Schneider, "Why Are Shirt Buttons On Different Sides For Men and Women?" *Mental Floss*, June 10, 2015, https://www.mentalfloss.com/article/64666/why-are-shirt-buttons-different-sides-men-and-women.

15   Iva Irene Sell, "Clothes for the Pre-School Child," *Journal of Home Economics* 20, no. 7 (July 1928): 477.

16   See, for example, Howard A. Rusk and Eugene J. Taylor, *Living with a Disability* (New York: The Blakiston Company, Inc., 1953), 38–9; Cookman and Zimmerman, *Functional Fashions for the Physically Handicapped*, 26.

17   Sven Raphael Schneider, "The Norfolk Jacket Guide—History, Style & How to Buy," *Gentlemen's Gazette*, April 5, 2013, www.gentlemansgazette.com/norfolk-jacket-guide.

18   "Rudy's Draws Fashion Crowd," *The News-Democrat*, March 11, 1926, 14.

19   J.W. Knapp Co., "October Sale of Dresses," *Lansing State Journal*, October 23, 1928, 5; Chas A. Stevens & Bros, "A Fashion Value Event! Sleeveless Frocks of Silk Pique: The Outstanding Summer Fashion," *Chicago Daily Tribune*, June 18, 1929, 7.

20   "Finds of the Fortnight," *Vogue* 87, no. 11 (June 1936): 89.

21   Clarice L. Scott, "Clothing Needs of Physically Handicapped Homemakers," *Journal of Home Economics* 51, no. 8 (October 1959): 710.

22   Scott, "Clothing Needs of Physically Handicapped Homemakers," 711.

about the line included a write-in option for readers to buy a pattern that the authors advertised for non-disabled women in athletic terms. "Here's a pattern for sports-loving separates based on Clarice Scott's research findings. It's ideal for bowling, golfing, or hiking. The shirt has underarm pleats for swinging, and the skirt smartly wraps in front or back."[23] Action pleats had moved from activewear to accessibility, and back again.

SPORTS GIRDLES

Lycra emerged out of DuPont chemistry labs. In 1955, the company decided to try it first on women's girdles, after their enormous success in the undergarments market with nylon stockings. Lycra was a synthetic fiber made to replace, and improve upon, rubber. Unlike rubberized elastic thread, Lycra did not deteriorate from perspiration; it was both lighter and stronger, and it could be dyed as well as machine washed and dried.[24] DuPont marketed Lycra girdles as ideal for women's sports. "At last, a girdle that lets you golf, bowl, ski—do any sport in utter comfort!"[25]

Salespersons were trained on talking points about the discomfort of sitting down—itself a disability issue, particularly for wheelchair users.[26] But women had mixed feelings about the idea of "comfort" in foundation-wear. The purpose of girdles was to shape and hide the wearer's body in order to create specific silhouettes—silhouettes that zippers had brought closer to the body. It was a new and groundbreaking concept for the body to shape clothing, and not the other way around.

In subsequent years, girdles for disability did not use Lycra. Designer Helen Cookman and occupational therapist Muriel Zimmerman recommended that disabled women instead look for the "two-way stretch girdle," an earlier style that used elastic to create more give, or to look toward maternity designs.[27] And in disabled designer Van Davis Odell's "Fashion-Able" brand, her girdle used "Lastex,"—a form of rubber thread introduced in the 1930s.[28]

SPEED SUITS

Lycra may not have succeeded in girdles, but it did introduce the idea that clothing could be fastened without closures at all. In effect, the garment itself *was* the closure. In 1975, sportswear designer Vera Maxwell debuted her "Speed Suit." The top was made of elastic jersey that hugged the wearer's torso. The top was sewn onto the skirt, creating a garment that appeared to be two pieces but was just one. The skirt came in different patterns and fabric, such as suede, silk, and cotton, and buyers could pick both their desired skirt and sleeve lengths. A scoop neck allowed women to slip the dress more easily and quickly—in as few as "seventeen seconds."[29]

"One wonders if the fabric has been injected with a miracle drug that gives the swimmer added strength."

— 23
Sue Smith, "These Fashions are Easy to Wear," *The Nebraska Farmer*, August 5, 1961, 54.

— 24
Kaori O'Connor, *Lycra: How a Fiber Shaped America* (New York: Routledge, 2011), 88.

25
O'Connor, *Lycra*, 95.

26
O'Connor, *Lycra*, 97.

— 27
Cookman and Zimmerman, *Functional Fashions for the Physically Handicapped*, 23.

28
Edward W. Lowman and Howard A. Rusk, "Self-Help Devices: Apparel for Handicapped Women," *Postgraduate Medicine* 35, no. 5 (May 1964): 551.

29
Eugenia Shephard, "Olympic Uniforms Inspire Vera Maxwell's 'Speed Suit,'" *The Blade*, March 11, 1975.

Sally Kirkland, former fashion editor at *Vogue* and *Life* magazines, gave the dress its name. Its speed came from the fact that there were no fastenings. The logo on the dress tag visualized forward movement, with the words appearing in an italic slant and lines behind the letters to animate their motion. "Vera Maxwell's 'speed suit' is designed to pop on in a zip (without one)," read one report, and "there isn't a sign of a button, a zipper, or a hook and eye," read another.[30]

Maxwell's inspiration for the garment came from the German women's Olympic uniforms worn for the first time at the 1972 Summer Olympics. This was the debut of the skinsuit. The first models were made of a fine cotton, that when wet, were virtually transparent, reprising a centuries-old fear about women's swimwear and modesty.[31] One year later, at the Yugoslavia World Swimming Championships, the East German team set seven world records and won ten out of fourteen events. West Germany responded with Dr. Conrad Dottinger's so-called "Belgrade suit." It was similarly high-necked and low-backed but made of Lycra. Prior suits were made of nylon and women's suits had skirts. Maxwell saw the seconds sliced off the swimmers' times and applied the same principle to dressing.[32] It was no surprise that Maxwell found inspiration from athletics, as one biographer wrote, "The former ballet dancer remains physically active, enjoying skiing, ice skating, and swimming."[33]

As the world reeled from the East German team's dominance, one 1974 *Sports Illustrated* article speculated, "One wonders if the fabric has been injected with a miracle drug that gives the swimmer added strength."[34] But as the Berlin doping trials laid bare in 1998 and 2000, the women were forced to take steroids as part of a state-sponsored doping program.[35] The athletes were never told about side-effects, despite being well-known to the trainers and doctors. Many women suffered long-term consequences to their own health, and some gave birth to disabled children. In this case, disability came at the very cost of speed.

One year after Maxwell released her "Speed Suit," she noted that the absence of fastenings made it ideal "for anyone whose fingers were crippled with arthritis," and several journalists discussed the design within the context of other garments for disability.[36] Fastenings had always proved a fundamental challenge to accessibility in clothing, and Maxwell saw Lycra's potential to radically upend this issue.

Vera Maxwell was not the only individual inspired by a moment of competition—however fraught. Throughout recent history, tournaments have prompted technological advances, which in turn have precipitated sporting successes. In 1978 Anne Kernaleguen wrote in *Clothing Designs for the Handicapped* that "quite a number of handicapped people have become actively involved in sports that years ago were deemed out of reach for them. At the same time, great advances have been made in sportswear that features functional lines."[37]

In a section titled "Sportswear for the Handicapped" she outlined the properties that made these features functional: that garments should facilitate ease of movement around the wearer's arms, neck, legs, and shoulders; that items for wheelchair sports should support the upper torso; that garments should be more durable around areas of significant wear such as the seat, knees, and elbows; that garments be made of natural fibers to increase absorption of perspiration; that the garment be both comfortable and easy to put on and take off.

But in 1978, when Kernaleguen's words were published, the Paralympics was celebrating its thirtieth anniversary, the Special Olympics was in its tenth year, and the Deaflympics had been running for fifty-four years. Across all of these competitions, women had been involved from the beginning. At the first Stoke Mandeville Games, or what would become the Paralympics, two women out of a group of sixteen took part in an archery competition. In the 1924 Deaflympics, just one woman competed. Even before that, when women first participated in the Olympics in 1900, British tennis champion Charlotte Cooper became the first individual champion. She lost her hearing in 1897. Disabled athletes had long been participating in sports, then. What was new, in 1978, was the attention paid to the way their clothing served them. That, in the end, was the slow part.

30

"Maxwell's Latest: The 'Speed Suit,'" *The Morning Call*, March 5, 1975; Shephard, "Olympic Uniforms'"

31

Patricia Campbell Warner, "Bathing and Swimming: Seeking a Sensible Costume," and "Women Enter the Olympics: A Sleeker Swimsuit," in *When the Girls Came Out to Play: The Birth of American Sports wear* (Amherst: University of Massachusetts Press, 2006), 61-103.

35

Lucas Aykroyd, "Health consequences of PEDs continue to plague ex-East German athletes," *Global Sport Matters*, November 7, 2019, www.globalsportmatters.com/health/2019/11/07/ex-east-german-athletes-struggle-with-health-problems-due-to-the-consequences-of-ped-taking.

32

"One-Piece 'Speed Suit,'" *The Washington Star*, January 4, 1976.

33

"Maxwell, Vera (Huppé)," *Current Biography*, 1977, 293.

34

Jule Campbell, "Light, Tight and Right for Racing," *Sports Illustrated*, August 12, 1974, www.vault.si.com/vault/1974/08/12/light-tight-and-right-for-racing.

36

Betty Ommerman, "Fashionable Clothes for Handicapped," *Central New Jersey Home News*, August 12, 1976.

37

Anne Kernaleguen, *Clothing Designs for the Handicapped* (Edmonton: University of Alberta Press, 1978), 14-15.

index

essayist bios

dal chodha

Dal Chodha is a London-based writer and consultant. He is Editor-in-Chief of *Archivist Addendum*, Contributing Editor at *Wallpaper** magazine, and he contributes to titles including *Modern Matter*, *i-D*, and *Encens*. Chodha is Pathway Leader of the BA Fashion Communication & Promotion course at Central Saint Martins. In 2020 he released his first book, *SHOW NOTES*, an original hybrid of journalism, poetry, and provocation. His second, *You gotta keep your head straight about clothes*, was released in December 2023.

michelle millar fisher

Michelle Millar Fisher is the Wornick Curator of Contemporary Decorative Arts at the Museum of Fine Arts, Boston. Previously, she worked at MoMA, the Philadelphia Museum of Art, and the Guggenheim Museum. Her work focuses on the intersections of people, power, and the material world. She leads an independent team on a book, touring exhibition, and program series called "Designing Motherhood: Things That Make and Break Our Births."

heather radke

Heather Radke is an essayist, journalist, and contributing editor, and reporter at Radiolab. She has written for publications including *The Believer*, *Time* Magazine, and *The Paris Review*, and she teaches at Columbia University's creative writing MFA Program. Her first book, *Butts: A Backstory*, was named one of the best books of 2022 by *Amazon*, *Esquire*, *Time*, and *Publisher's Weekly*.

samantha n. sheppard

Samantha N. Sheppard is an Associate Professor of Cinema and Media Studies and the Chair of the Department of Performing and Media Arts at Cornell University. She is the author and co-editor of several books, including *Sporting Blackness: Race, Embodiment, and Critical Muscle Memory on Screen* (2020). In 2021, Dr. Sheppard was named an Academy Film Scholar by the Academy of Motion Picture Arts and Sciences.

natalie e. wright

Natalie E. Wright is a historian of design and disability and a doctoral candidate of Design History at the University of Wisconsin-Madison. Her work has been supported by the Social Sciences and Humanities Research Council of Canada and the Smithsonian American Art Museum, amongst others. Wright's writing has appeared in *Material Intelligence* magazine, where she is also a contributing editor, and the journal *Dress*. She has held curatorial positions at institutions across the United States and Canada, where she trained in object-based research.

acknowledgments

A project like this requires perseverance. First and foremost that of athletes, past and present, who have pushed against their challenges and toward their goals. Their stories enthrall the world and inform our views. At Nike, dedication to listening to the athlete is a 50+ year charge. Striving to execute on their behalf underpins the company's mission.

Similarly, preparing a book of this scale requires a collective spirit and unwavering patience. We'd like to thank Chloe Scheffe and Natalie Shields for their vision, curiosity, and determination. We're grateful to Brenna Olenginski, Demetria White, Emily Favret, Jenna Golden, Kate Meyers, KeJuan Wilkens, Sara Blasing, and Taunya Woo for their support in research and development. We are indebted to Nike's designers, Tania Flynn, Caitlin Kis, Flavia Cervantes, Valentina Azizova, Emily Drake, Lisa Mechanic, Tara Sweeney, Bridget Monroe, Jessica Laird, Emily Polkow, Raffaella Barbey, Maris Mitchell, Katie Bahr, Jordie Katcher, Charlotte Harris, and Martha Moore, for all their insights. For the time and energy spent facilitating our conversations, we thank Jordan Talley, Adam Sutton, Kate Borowicz, Kris Briggs, Erica Parker, Ryan Bobier, Richard Sharma, Lori Roth, Melissa Callender, Oscar Garcia, Sara Gendernalik, and Nya Mason. Special recognition is due to the Department of Nike Archives. We thank Jack O'Brien and Cass O'Brien for their support and patience through many late nights, and subsequent early mornings. For shaping the lenses through which this book looks at apparel, we thank essayists Dal Chodha, Samantha N. Sheppard, Heather Radke, Michelle Millar Fisher, and Natalie E. Wright. And above all, we thank athletes Chandra Cheeseborough, Joan Benoit Samuelson, Sha'Carri Richardson, Dina Asher-Smith, Anna Cockrell, Megan Rapinoe, Dawn Staley, Rayssa Leal, Scout Bassett, Deyna Castellanos, Shelly-Ann Fraser-Pryce, Xochilt Hoover, Naomi Osaka, Caster Semenya, Sue Bird, Tatyana McFadden, and Kirsty Godso, for all the stories they so generously shared with us. Thank you.

picture credits

phaidon press limited
2 cooperage yard
london e15 2qr

phaidon.com

phaidon press inc.
111 broadway
new york, ny 10006

first published 2024
© 2024 Nike, Inc

isbn 978 1 83866 907 2

commissioning editor
emilia terragni

project editors
robyn taylor
david tibbs
phoebe stephenson

production controller
adela cory

text contributor
maisie skidmore

design
scheffe shields

typefaces
filesofia, union, yorick

Printed in China